ROYAL

THE 145TH OPEN
Card of the Championship Course

Hole	Par	Yards	Hole	Par	Yards
1	4	367	10	4	451
2	4	390	11	4	482
3	4	377	12	4	430
4	5	555	13	4	473
5	3	209	14	3	178
6	5	601	15	4	499
7	4	401	16	5	554
8	3	123	17	3	220
9	4	422	18	4	458
Out	36	3,445	In	35	3,745
			Total	71	7,190

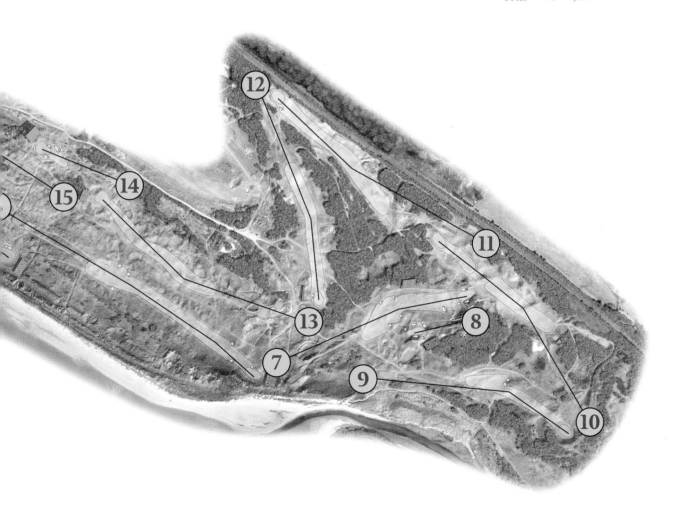

Aurum Press
74-77 White Lion Street, London N1 9PF

Published 2016 by Aurum Press

Copyright 2016 R&A Championships Limited

Course illustration by Strokesaver

Project coordinator: Sarah Wooldridge
Additional thanks to NTT Data

A CIP catalogue record for this book is available
from the British Library

ISBN-13: 978 1 78131 661 0

Designed and produced by Davis Design
Colour retouching by Luciano Retouching Services, Inc.
Printed in Slovenia by Svet Print d.o.o.

THE OPEN

145TH ROYAL TROON

EDITOR
Andy Farrell

WRITERS AND PHOTOGRAPHERS

Writers	Getty Images	The R&A	Golf Editors
Peter Dixon	Andrew Redington	Ross Kinnaird	Steve Rose
Andy Farrell	Stuart Franklin	David Cannon	Dan Istitene
John Hopkins	Matthew Lewis	Warren Little	Mark Trowbridge
Lewine Mair	Mike Ehrmann	Jan Kruger	Richard Martin-Roberts
Art Spander	Kevin Cox	Richard Heathcote	Rob Harborne
Alistair Tait		Tom Dulat	

Foreword

By Henrik Stenson

Looking back now, even after all the wonderful messages of congratulations, seeing the video and reading the accounts that follow here, it is still hard to take in everything that happened over those four incredible days at Royal Troon. Simply to win The Open, especially as a European, was a dream come true, but the manner and significance of it could never have been imagined.

To beat a competitor like Phil Mickelson, one of the best to play the game, makes it even more special. We both played some great golf and I knew he wasn't going to back down at any point so I had to keep pushing all the way to the end.

I feel very privileged to be the first Swede to hold the Claret Jug. There have been many great players from my country who have tried in past years with some close calls, Jesper Parnevik in particular twice. He sent me a message, "Go out and finish what I didn't manage to finish."

There are so many people to thank, including The R&A for staging such a wonderful Championship, the greenkeeping staff at Royal Troon for preparing an immaculate links and the great fans who braved all the elements of the British summer. Thanks, too, of course, to my family and my team, including caddie Gareth Lord and coach Pete Cowen, for all their support and hard work.

Not that I was going to shout about it, but that week I felt it was going to be my turn. On the Wednesday we heard my dear friend Mike Gerbich had passed away. Mike was a real good guy from Dubai, a keen golfer and a big supporter of mine in good days and bad days. I felt like he was there with me all week. This one's for you, Mike.

The Championship Committee

CHAIRMAN
Peter Unsworth

DEPUTY CHAIRMAN
Clive Brown

COMMITTEE

Stuart Allison	Nick Ellis
Peter Arthur	John Louden
Andrew Bathurst	Charlie Maran
David Boyle	Paul McKellar
Peter Cowell	David Meacher

CHIEF EXECUTIVE
Martin Slumbers

EXECUTIVE DIRECTOR – CHAMPIONSHIPS
Johnnie Cole-Hamilton

EXECUTIVE DIRECTOR – RULES AND EQUIPMENT STANDARDS
David Rickman

Introduction

By Peter Unsworth
Chairman of the Championship Committee of The R&A

The 145th Open at Royal Troon will be remembered for one of the finest performances in the final round of a Major Championship. During a gripping duel with 2013 Champion Golfer of the Year Phil Mickelson, Henrik Stenson gave a masterly display to win by three strokes to become Champion Golfer of the Year and Sweden's first ever male Major Champion.

The R&A introduced a number of successful initiatives for this year's Championship. A new Camping Village proved to be very popular among those aged 25 and under who enjoyed a stay at the free campsite. A new nine hole championship was held shortly before The Open as part of our efforts to promote nine hole golf as a quick and enjoyable form of the game. We also introduced Twilight Tickets from 4pm on Thursday and Friday of the Championship at a reduced price.

The 145th Open offered the most comprehensive television and digital coverage in the Championship's history. There are now more ways to watch and listen to The Open across a wide variety of digital, radio and television channels, including our new broadcast partners Sky and NBC.

There are so many people who deserve a huge amount of praise and credit for delivering The Open to world class standards. I wish to thank Royal Troon Championship Committee, the staff at both Royal Troon Golf Club and the Ladies' Golf Club, Troon and the many hundreds of volunteers who work tirelessly before and during the Championship to ensure its smooth running.

The 145th Open was my last as Chairman of the Championship Committee and I wish my successor Clive Brown the very best as we look forward to Royal Birkdale in 2017.

Peter M.G. Unsworth

Lee Westwood

Haydn Porteous

Paul Dunne

Colin Montgomerie

145TH
ROYAL TROON

AMERICA

FedEx St Jude Classic	9-12 June
Steve Stricker, USA	
Brian Gay, USA	
Russell Henley, USA	
Seung Yul Noh, Korea	
Quicken Loans National	23-26 June
Billy Hurley III, USA	
Vijay Singh, Fiji	
Jon Rahm, Spain	
Harold Varner III, USA	
Barracuda Championship	30 June - 3 July
Greg Chalmers, Australia	

THE
OPEN®
QUALIFYING SERIES

AFRICA

Joberg Open	14-17 Jan
Haydn Porteous, South Africa	
Zander Lombard, South Africa	
Anthony Wall, England	

Nicolas Colsaerts   *Kodai Ichihara*   *Steve Stricker*   *Matthew Southgate*

EUROPE

Nordea Masters   2-5 June
Lasse Jensen, Denmark

100th Open de France   30 June - 3 July
Brandon Stone, South Africa
Alex Noren, Sweden
Callum Shinkwin, England
Richard Sterne, South Africa

Aberdeen Asset Management
Scottish Open   7-10 July
Tyrrell Hatton, England
Nicolas Colsaerts, Belgium
Matteo Manassero, Italy
Richie Ramsay, Scotland

FINAL QUALIFYING

Gailes Links   28 June
Oskar Arvidsson, Sweden
Scott Fernandez, Spain
Colin Montgomerie, Scotland

Hillside   28 June
Jack Senior, England
Paul Howard[(P)], England
Dave Coupland[(P)], England

Royal Cinque Ports   28 June
Matthew Southgate, England
Steven Alker, New Zealand
James Heath, England

Woburn   28 June
Paul Dunne, Republic of Ireland
Ryan Evans, England
Robert Rock[(P)], England

[(P)]Qualified after play-off

JAPAN

Mizuno Open   26-29 May
Kodai Ichihara, Japan
Shugo Imahira, Japan
Sang-hee Lee, Korea
Hideto Tanihara, Japan

THAILAND

Thailand Golf Championship   10-13 Dec
Jamie Donaldson, Wales
Clément Sordet, France
Lee Westwood, England
Phachara Khongwatmai, Thailand

AUSTRALIA

Emirates Australian Open   26-29 Nov
Matthew Jones, Australia
Rod Pampling, Australia
Nick Cullen, Australia

EXEMPT COMPETITORS

Shane Lowry

Dustin Johnson

Sergio Garcia

Rickie Fowler

Mark O'Meara

Name, Country	Category
Byeong Hun An, Korea	4,5,6
Kiradech Aphibarnrat, Thailand	4,5
Steven Bowditch, Australia	12,14
Keegan Bradley, USA	10
Kristoffer Broberg, Sweden	5
Rafa Cabrera Bello, Spain	4
Mark Calcavecchia, USA	1
Paul Casey, England	4,12
Kevin Chappell, USA	4
Darren Clarke, Northern Ireland	1,2
George Coetzee, South Africa	17
Ben Curtis, USA	1
John Daly, USA	1
Marco Dawson, USA	21
Jason Day, Australia	3,4,10,11,12,14
Luke Donald**, England	4
Victor Dubuisson, France	5
Jason Dufner, USA	10
David Duval, USA	1
Ernie Els, South Africa	1,2
Harris English, USA	12
Tony Finau, USA	4
Ross Fisher, England	5
Matthew Fitzpatrick, England	4,5
Tommy Fleetwood, England	5
Rickie Fowler, USA	4,11,12,14
Marcus Fraser**, Australia	4
Jim Furyk, USA	4,12
Sergio Garcia, Spain	3,4
Fabian Gomez, Argentina	4
Branden Grace, South Africa	4,5,14
Scott Gregory*, England	22
Emiliano Grillo, Argentina	4
Bill Haas, USA	4,12,14
James Hahn, USA	4
Todd Hamilton, USA	1
Padraig Harrington, Rep of Ireland	1,2
Scott Hend, Australia	4
Jim Herman**, USA	4
Charley Hoffman, USA	4,12
Nathan Holman, Australia	16
JB Holmes, USA	4,12,14
Billy Horschel, USA	4
David Howell, England	5
Yuta Ikeda, Japan	20
Thongchai Jaidee, Thailand	4,5,14
Miguel Angel Jiménez, Spain	5
Dustin Johnson, USA	4,8,12,14
Zach Johnson, USA	1,2,3,4,12,14
Andrew Johnston, England	7
Rikard Karlberg, Sweden	7
Smylie Kaufman, USA	13
Martin Kaymer, Germany	5,8,11
KT Kim, Korea	4,19
Chris Kirk, USA	14
Kevin Kisner, USA	4,12
Patton Kizzire, USA	4
Søren Kjeldsen, Denmark	4,5

Name, Country	Category
Colt Knost**, USA	4
Russell Knox, Scotland	4
Satoshi Kodaira, Japan	18
Matt Kuchar, USA	4,12,14
Anirban Lahiri, India	5,14,15
Paul Lawrie, Scotland	1
Danny Lee, New Zealand	4,12,14
Soomin Lee, Korea	7
Marc Leishman, Australia	3,4,14
Justin Leonard, USA	1
David Lingmerth, Sweden	4
Jamie Lovemark**, USA	4
Shane Lowry, Rep of Ireland	4,5
Joost Luiten, Netherlands	7
Sandy Lyle, Scotland	1
Hideki Matsuyama, Japan	4,12,14
Stefano Mazzoli*, Italy	24
Graeme McDowell, Northern Ireland	4
William McGirt, USA	13
Rory McIlroy, Northern Ireland	1,2,4,5,6,10,12
Phil Mickelson, USA	1,2,4,14
Yusaku Miyazato, Japan	19
Francesco Molinari, Italy	4
Ryan Moore, USA	4
James Morrison, England	5
Kevin Na, USA	4,12
Jordan Niebrugge, USA	3
Thorbjørn Olesen, Denmark	5
Mark O'Meara, USA	1
Louis Oosthuizen, South Africa	1,2,3,4,5,12,14
Ryan Palmer, USA	4
Scott Piercy, USA	12
Thomas Pieters, Belgium	5
Patrick Reed, USA	4,5,12,14
Justin Rose, England	3,4,5,8,12
Charl Schwartzel, South Africa	4,5,14
Adam Scott, Australia	3,4,9,14
Webb Simpson, USA	8
Brandt Snedeker, USA	4,12
Jordan Spieth, USA	3,4,8,9,12,14
Brendan Steele, USA	4
Henrik Stenson, Sweden	4,5,12
Robert Streb, USA	12
Andy Sullivan, England	4,5
Daniel Summerhays**, USA	4
Justin Thomas, USA	4
Yosuke Tsukada, Japan	20
Jimmy Walker, USA	4,12,14
Jeunghun Wang, Korea	4
Marc Warren, Scotland	5
Bubba Watson, USA	4,9,12,14
Lee Westwood, England	4
Bernd Wiesberger, Austria	4,5
Danny Willett, England	3,4,5,9
Chris Wood, England	5,6
Gary Woodland, USA	4

*Denotes amateur   **Denotes reserve

KEY TO EXEMPTIONS FROM THE OPEN QUALIFYING SERIES

Exemptions for 2016 were granted to the following:

(1) The Open Champions aged 60 or under on 17 July 2016.

(2) The Open Champions for 2006-2015.

(3) First 10 and anyone tying for 10th place in The 2015 Open Championship at St Andrews.

(4) The first 50 players on the Official World Golf Ranking for Week 21, 2016, with additional players and reserves drawn from the highest ranked non-exempt players in the weeks prior to The Open.

(5) First 30 in the Race to Dubai Rankings for 2015.

(6) The BMW PGA Championship winners for 2014-2016.

(7) First 5 European Tour members and any European Tour members tying for 5th place, not otherwise exempt, in the top 20 of the Race to Dubai on completion of the 2016 BMW International Open.

(8) The US Open Champions for 2012-2016.

(9) The Masters Tournament Champions for 2012-2016.

(10) The PGA Champions for 2011-2015.

(11) The PLAYERS Champions for 2014-2016.

(12) The leading 30 qualifiers for the 2015 TOUR CHAMPIONSHIP.

(13) First 5 PGA TOUR members and any PGA TOUR members tying for 5th place, not exempt in the top 20 of the PGA TOUR FedExCup Points List for 2016 on completion of the 2016 Quicken Loans National.

(14) Playing members of the 2015 Presidents Cup Teams.

(15) First and anyone tying for 1st place on the Order of Merit of the Asian Tour for 2015.

(16) First and anyone tying for 1st place on the Order of Merit of the Tour of Australasia for 2015.

(17) First and anyone tying for 1st place on the Order of Merit of the Southern Africa PGA Sunshine Tour for 2015.

(18) The Japan Open Champion for 2015.

(19) First 2 and anyone tying for 2nd place, on the Official Money List of the Japan Golf Tour for 2015.

(20) First 2 and anyone tying for 2nd place, not exempt having applied OQS Japan in a cumulative money list taken from all official 2016 Japan Golf Tour events up to and including the 2016 Japan Tour Championship.

(21) The Senior Open Champion for 2015.

(22) The Amateur Champion for 2016.

(23) The US Amateur Champion for 2015.

(24) The International European Amateur Champion for 2015.

(25) The Mark H McCormack Medal (Men's World Amateur Golf Ranking™) winner for 2015.

Seaside Golf at Its Best

By Andy Farrell

When The Open returns to Royal Troon, as it did for a ninth time in 2016, it shows the Championship retains its philopatric tendency.

It may have found a spiritual home at St Andrews, but returning to its birthplace is more than a sentimental exercise — especially given The 145th Open, in the thrilling weekend duel between Henrik Stenson and Phil Mickelson, provided us with one of the greatest finishes of all.

Prestwick, created by Old Tom Morris, staged the first Open Championship in 1860, in fact the first 12, and 24 in all before the course was outgrown by the scale of the event in the 1920s. It was then that neighbouring Troon took over as a representative for this most charming, and underrated, stretch of golfing linksland on the banks of the Firth of Clyde, which includes such gems as Prestwick St Nicholas, Dundonald Links and Gailes Links.

As The Open has become ever bigger, fortunately Troon has remained a mighty enough test, and has enough land, to host the most modern of Championships. In fact, the course has played a key role in its evolution.

Troon Golf Club was founded in 1878 and developed on land to the south of the town, eventually expanding to 18 holes with the ninth green just the other side of Pow Burn from the Prestwick links. By the start of the 1900s, courses lined much of this stretch of the Ayrshire coast. Bernard Darwin wrote of journeying from Glasgow: "As one approaches Prestwick, the train seems to be voyaging through one endless and continuous golf course."

The gently curving coastline can be a sheltered idyll with views of Arran and the Kintyre hills, as well as the Ailsa Craig. On such days the setting has its own charm, although there are plenty of days it is exposed to the full furies from the Atlantic, as the best players in the world experienced for themselves. Whatever the weather, here lies "a proud, rigorous links, seaside golf at its best," as the authors of the *Shell International Encyclopaedia of Golf* declared.

Charlie Hunter, the greenkeeper from Prestwick who had been an apprentice under Old Tom, set down the original six-hole layout. The rigour was provided over the years by two of its earliest professionals, George Strath, of the St Andrews

No first tee on any Open venue is as near to the sea as Royal Troon's is to the town's South Beach.

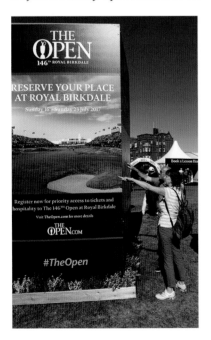

golfing family, and Willie Fernie, the Champion Golfer of the Year in 1883. Fernie it was who created two of the most dramatic holes on the course, the short but perilous eighth, the Postage Stamp, and the longer but also dangerous 11th, the Railway.

James Braid, the five-time Champion Golfer of the Year, made some improvements prior to Troon's first Open in 1923, won by Arthur Havers, and more recent renovations have been carried out by Tom Mackenzie and Martin Ebert.

Having studied extensive archive material about the course, the latter duo's work has seen only a handful of yards added to the layout, but many old features that were lost over time — and following the use of the links as a testing ground for tanks during World War II — restored. The first part of the 15th fairway has been moved to the left to aid logistics but also to bring back a former version of the hole. Trees behind the ninth green have been cleared and a spectacular new tee at the 10th added.

Proud to be a pioneering Open Camper

Rising with the sun, the perfect wake-up call at 5.30am, we trundled across a freshly mown field into the biggest golfing event in the world.

In my wellies and puffer jacket I felt slightly at odds with those who had actually paid (an arm and a leg) for a carpeted hotel room. But that was the beauty of it. I felt proud to be an Open Camper, a pioneer of this new and innovative scheme. It brought a fresh dimension to golf that is forward thinking and extremely inclusive.

For young golf fans, The R&A's free campsite greeted them with open arms. For the first time ever, The Open offered free accommodation to anyone under 25 and families with young children.

As for the camping itself, for a week spent outdoors on the chiselled coastline of a Scottish Links, it felt highly appropriate. I will forever associate golf spectating with countryside camping — an affinity not unknown to previous golf fans but, I hope, increasingly common in years to come.

There was no mistaking the purpose of those who were there. There was a real camaraderie between the campers, sport once again bridging gaps between strangers.

With the day's play screened in the rugby club bar, the centre of the campsite, and food served throughout the day, golf was the only topic of conversation — and everyone had something to say.

Unlike a hotel, the campsite appeared an extension of the event, a short walk from one tented village to another — no cars, no buses, no hotels. We were a stitch in a multi-coloured patchwork and closer to the action than we ever hoped to be.

With brand new tents, food on site and fantastic living facilities, like Stenson's chip onto the 16th green in the final round, the idea was pitched perfectly. As first-time Open visitors, we would never have got to see the one without the other.

—*Rebecca Dixon*

What has never changed at Troon is the quality of the greens. Darwin noted that they were "smooth and true, and of an almost velvety consistency." Bobby Locke agreed. Following his victory in 1950 he sent the club an annual Christmas card with the message: "Best wishes for this year and the future. Still the best greens in the world." After all the putts they holed this year, Stenson and Mickelson could only concur.

With a combination of the weather over the previous few months and a lot of hard work by the greenkeeping staff, the links could not have been presented in better condition. The record scoring that resulted in The 145th Open was a testament

to, rather than a denigration of, the layout.

Any course that has one of the longest holes on The Open rota, the 601-yard sixth, and the shortest, the 123-yard eighth, must be approached with all manner of strategies. There is not simply one way, as the club's motto makes clear: *Tam Arte Quam Marte*, or "As much by skill as by strength."

Arnold Palmer said something similar, but in his own way, when he explained that he could not allow himself "to get locked into a life and death struggle with the course."

Picking his moment to attack during The Open in 1962, Palmer took on the Railway hole with a succession of long-iron shots, while Jack Nicklaus,

Danny Willett practises from a bunker at the perilous Postage Stamp.

Time for nine

Nine hole golf was showcased at Royal Troon as a group of 30 amateurs, both men and women, took part in a new championship staged by The R&A on the weekend prior to The 145th Open. The event was part of a campaign to promote nine hole golf as a quick and enjoyable way to play, both socially or competitively.

Competitors played the first five holes of The Open course and then the closing stretch from the 15th home, with Denis Gaffney and John Prendergast, of the Island Golf Club, Dublin, emerging as the overall winners.

"John and I had a wonderful time today," said Gaffney. "Just to come here was the prize, never mind winning the competition.

"It was our first time here and this is also the first time we've played in a nine hole competition. People will find nine hole golf handy in the evenings and the weekends. It's great for the game."

the newly crowned US Open champion, suffered a 10 at the hole. *Country Life*'s Pat Ward-Thomas was left with an indelible memory. "I will never forget," he wrote, "the sight of Palmer's rifling second shots, with a one or two-iron, that subdued the hole as no one else in the world could have done."

On a traditional out-and-back links, with a loop around the turn, the course starts gently but has a real sting coming home. Both Mickelson and Stenson separated themselves from their rivals by taming the second nine as rarely seen before. Yet it took a supreme display of long-iron play by the Swede to end America's run of six successive victories at the venue.

Walter Hagen might have won Troon's first Open but for English professional Havers holing a bunker shot at the 18th. Instead, Palmer set the ball rolling for the Americans with his six-stroke victory. This was a significant moment for The Open, such was the American's popularity. So large was the gallery who wanted to see him retain his title, many gained access from the beach and overwhelmed the links. Subsequently, all arrangements for stewarding and spectator control had to be upgraded. The modern Open was born.

Rory McIlroy drives from the spectacular new tee at the 10th hole with the town of Prestwick behind.

Tom Weiskopf led from start to finish to become the last winner to use the old small ball in 1973 and, after the club achieved Royal status on its centenary, Tom Watson won his fourth Open title in 1982. He was helped this time by the collapses of Bobby Clampett, who was seven ahead before an eight at the sixth in the third round, and Nick Price, who lost a two-shot lead on the closing holes.

Mark Calcavecchia won The Open in 1989 in the first four-hole play-off, beating Australians Greg Norman and Wayne Grady. Norman set the course record of 64 — only usurped this year by Mickelson and then Stenson — in the final round, but when he went out of bounds at the last in the play-off, Calcavecchia hit a wonderful five-iron to six feet to seal his only Major victory.

Darren Clarke and Jesper Parnevik were the men denied as Justin Leonard came from five behind with an immaculate putting display in 1997, while the unheralded Todd Hamilton felled Ernie Els in a play-off in 2004. Ignoring the South African's power game, Hamilton plotted his way round the course, using a hybrid club from the tee and the fairway, as well as for chipping around the greens.

There have been few theories about America's dominance at Troon but Graeme McDowell came up with one. "It's very American around the greens," he said. "It's actually not very linksy. The ball rolls off into the semi-rough and you get the opportunity to chip with a lot of loft. It's quite unusual."

One player who undoubtedly conquered Troon through guile and precision was Joyce Wethered, who won the British Ladies' Championship here in 1925. In beating the American Glenna Collett in the third round she holed a long putt at the 11th

Trains still pass along the 11th, the Railway hole, but no longer halt as putts are taken.

which provided a postscript to the famous "What train?" incident at Sheringham earlier in her career. "It was at this point that I again lived up to my curious reputation for not noticing trains," recalled Wethered, who was the very antithesis of Colin Montgomerie.

"This time I was more fully aware of the reality of the train in question. It was puffing smoke in clouds behind the green in a way that could not very well be ignored. However, I was too well acquainted with the ways of a Scotch engine driver not to know that he was determined to see the hole played to a finish before he continued with his goods to Ayr. Knowing this, there was little to be gained by my waiting."

In the final, Wethered beat her formidable English rival Cecil Leitch in one of the great matches of any era. A huge gallery watched as Wethered recovered from being three down after 10 in the morning, took the lead in the afternoon, lost two late holes but finally won at the 37th. Darwin wrote: "Everyone who saw that match will always wish that there could for that year have been two queens on twin thrones of exactly equal splendour."

At the end of The 145th Open, a similar sentiment could have been expressed about two kings of the modern game.

ROYAL TROON CHAMPIONS

1923	Arthur Havers
1950	Bobby Locke
1962	Arnold Palmer
1973	Tom Weiskopf
1982	Tom Watson
1989	Mark Calcavecchia
1997	Justin Leonard
2004	Todd Hamilton
2016	Henrik Stenson

Monty a man about Troon

Lewine Mair rises early to see the town's favourite son start The Open

Though the star roles in The 145th Open belonged to Henrik Stenson and Phil Mickelson, there was some truly inspired casting at the start of the week.

The Reverend Stephen Willett, father of Danny, the Masters Champion, was chosen to say grace at the Association of Golf Writers' dinner on the Tuesday evening, while Colin Montgomerie was selected by The R&A to hit the first shot of the Championship on the Thursday morning.

The Reverend Willett's was a peak-time performance. Monty's, on the other hand, was anything but. Not, mind you, that anyone would have known as much from the size of crowd in position for his 6.35am start.

Troon's favourite son had spent plenty of time ahead of the event staying at his father's home in Troon. James Montgomerie was once the secretary at Royal Troon and Monty, at the age of four, had hit his first shots on the little practice course next to the Troon Ladies' clubhouse.

Across May, June and July, Montgomerie had watched the "Open city" coming to life and the golf course reaching what would be seen as a state of near perfection.

He would have liked an invitation to play in the Championship but, when none was forthcoming, the 53-year-old Scot headed for Final Qualifying at Glasgow Golf Club's Gailes Links. Though he had not played the course before, club officials happily extended the extra practice opportunities which contributed to his opening 66.

Monty's second round was an anti-climactic 71, which resulted in a two-hour wait to see if a five-under-par tally would make the grade. Instead of heading back to the family home, he sat in his car pondering on just how much he wanted to play one last Open at Troon; the next time around, he reasoned, he would be too old.

To his relief, he scraped in by a single stroke — and then came more good news as The R&A phoned to ask if he would like to hit the Championship's opening drive, one which would be televised live all around the world for the first time. Monty seized his chance, viewing it as a great honour for himself, his family and the Troon members.

Those who had stayed in bed in the hope of catching some extra sleep knew precisely who to blame when, at around 5am on the first day, Troon awoke to a chorus of alarm clocks and banging doors. No less than Monty himself, Monty-followers wanted to be there for the big moment.

It was shortly before 6.30 that the player, whose trio otherwise consisted of Marc Leishman and Luke Donald, walked onto the tee and into the warmth of a welcoming throng. Sensing something akin to the pressure of hitting the opening ball on a Ryder Cup morning, he unleashed a drive which was entirely in keeping with the occasion.

Wisely, the photographers stayed put, for the second shot disappeared into a bunker and, yes, this most sensitive of golfers had been disturbed. It was also in keeping that he knew precisely what the culprit had been doing — removing a plastic cover from wi-fi equipment in the stands overlooking the adjacent 18th fairway.

The ball was buried and, when Montgomerie failed to extricate it at the first time of asking, it rolled back into one of his footprints. A footprint which, he afterwards acknowledged, was always going to be "deeper than most."

At this point, he emerged to discuss the situation with Alastair McLean, his caddie. McLean, though, knew his master well enough to realise that this was one of those occasions when he would do better to say too little rather than too much.

Monty took it upon himself to play away from the hole with his fourth shot and the tactic worked. The ball made a triumphant exit and, a chip and a putt later, this seemingly omnipresent competitor-cum-commentator had his double-bogey. "If there's such a thing as a good double-bogey, that's it," he said.

Monty being Monty, he did not mind saying that the "blooming birdies" of his playing companions had served as a more than minor irritation. Equally, he made sure that everyone knew that he had finished the round leading both of them.

His concentration had slipped a tad when he heard the sizzle of bacon from a stand at the seventh, but McLean kept his player's nose to the proverbial grindstone as they turned in 33. They were home into the buffeting wind in an acceptable 38 and, thanks to how Monty had whipped the party round in almost exactly four hours, he enjoyed an elongated stint as one of the clubhouse leaders.

Things would not be so very different when he achieved his original ambition of playing down the 18th fairway on Sunday. He once again teed-off first — and he once again left the rest of the field for dead in terms of pace of play.

If his closing 76 was relatively lacklustre, his parting line was anything but. "For the second time this week," he beamed, "I'm the leader in the clubhouse."

The Putt That Would Not Drop

By Andy Farrell

Phil Mickelson has being getting things round the wrong way ever since he learnt to swing a golf club by mirroring the actions of his father.

The established protocol for succeeding at Royal Troon is to make a score on the easier outward half and hang on to it for dear life on the way home. A string of short par fours followed by two par fives make for a gentle start before the horrors of the back nine.

When Greg Norman set the course record of 64 in the final round of The Open in 1989, he birdied the first six holes. When Tiger Woods matched the Australian's score in the third round of The Open eight years later, he had halves of four-under-par and three-under-par respectively, the latter mainly thanks to an eagle at the 16th.

On a beautiful, if rare for July 2016, day of sunshine for the opening round of The 145th Open, what wind there was accentuated the differential with the two halves of the course colour-coded on

Phil Mickelson's putt at the 18th would not drop.

the scoreboard — red (birdies) for the first nine, blue (bogeys and worse) for the second nine.

As the afternoon progressed and the breeze fell away, however, Mickelson took advantage of his good fortune with the elements to dramatic effect. After going out in 32, the left-hander came home in 31 for a new course record of 63, eight-under-par.

Yet to the Champion Golfer of the Year in 2013, and everyone else watching, the number on the scorecard was one higher than it should have been. For certain, as his putt for birdie on the final green approached the hole, something even more historic was about to unfold. For the first time in any Major Championship someone was about to post a 62.

Only an act of the golfing gods, or perhaps some unseen imperfection on the turf, suddenly intervened. Mickelson's ball was diverted to the right, caught the edge of the hole but, its speed just too much for gravity to do its thing, it lipped out. Mickelson threw his head back in surprise, disappointment and sheer disbelief. Jim "Bones" Mackay, his caddie, threw himself backwards onto the ground. A gasp rang round the grandstands

In the first group of the day, Australia's Marc Leishman escapes with a par at the Postage Stamp after this bunker shot.

Tony Finau's first round in The Open was a 67.

that ordinarily would only accompany someone being robbed of the Claret Jug on the Sunday night of The Open.

"I thought it was in," Mickelson muttered as he walked off the green. "I can't believe I didn't do it."

This was the ninth 63 in The Open and the 28th in all Majors since Johnny Miller first posted the magical score at Oakmont in 1973. Norman, Woods, Jack Nicklaus and Nick Price all might have gone lower, but here the curse of 62 had struck again in particularly cruel fashion.

"It was one of the best rounds I've ever played, I was able to take advantage of the conditions, and yet I want to shed a tear right now," said the 46-year-old American, still visibly shaken by the experience. "That putt on 18 was an opportunity to do something historical. I knew it and with a foot to go I thought I had done it. I saw that ball rolling right in the centre.

"I went to get it out, I had that surge of adren-

"After a display such as this, it is remarkable to think that the five-time Major winner has not won a title of any description since breaking his Open duck in 2013 at Muirfield."

—James Corrigan,
The Daily Telegraph

"There was Mickelson, winner of The Open in 2013, putting himself in serious position after one day to win yet another of the Major Championships no one believed he ever would have a sniff at in the first place."

—Mark Cannizzaro,
New York Post

"Mickelson's round was sub-lime. He benefited from the increasingly benign conditions, literally the calm before the predicted storms and gave Troon its greatest Open day."

—Rick Broadbent,
The Times

"On a day when his love affair with Royal Troon was confirmed, Phil Mickelson said he discovered that he now believed in golf gods."

—Jim McCabe,
Golfweek

Germany's Martin Kaymer did not drop a stroke in his five-under-par opening round of 66.

aline that I had just shot 62, and then I had the heartbreak that I hadn't and watched as the ball lipped out. Wow, that stings."

It is not how a player who has opened up a three-stroke lead on the first day of The Open normally reacts, but the 145th version of the game's oldest Major had already reached an emotional high point. In somewhat more sedate fashion Patrick Reed had set the early pace with a 66 that matched the previous lowest score for an opening round at Troon, while Martin Kaymer, playing in Mickelson's wake, also reached five-under-par.

Eight of the top 11 on the leaderboard were Americans, with defending Champion Zach Johnson, veteran Steve Stricker, Open debutants Justin Thomas and Tony Finau, plus Keegan Bradley and Billy Horschel among those on 67. If this raised hopes Stateside of a seventh consecutive American winner at Troon, only

Patrick Reed holed out for an eagle-two at the third.

three times previously had the Stars and Stripes been at the top of the leaderboard after the first round of The Open at the famous Ayrshire links. Of those, only Tom Weiskopf in 1973 had gone on to win.

Reed was taking nothing for granted. "Honestly, with how competition is these days, it doesn't matter where you come from, you have to be on your game and stick to your game plan," he said. That was all the Texan was trying to do, but he received a nice bonus when he holed a wedge shot from 139 yards at the third hole for an eagle-two. With three birdies before the turn, he was out in 31 before returning home in level-par 35.

The difference between the two nines, Reed said, was, "David versus Goliath." He explained: "If you hit good tee shots it was playing pretty easy on the front nine, but it doesn't matter if the wind is blowing or not, that back nine is tough. Every hole seems to be over 470 yards and you get to the 17th, the par three, and it's 220."

A fine opening 68 for England's Justin Rose.

"It's one of those courses that allows you to get off to a quick start. You can get almost overconfident or cocky and so you could shoot 31-41. You have to stay humble on it, take your medicine if you hit a wayward shot, strategising to at least salvage bogey."

Even Colin Montgomerie, who as a local Royal Troon member had the honour of hitting the opening tee shot at 6.35am and being the first player announced by The Open's new starter David Lancaster, recovered from his double-bogey at the first hole to be out in three-under-par. And promptly came home in three-over-par.

Thomas, whose previous links experience extended to an appearance in the Alfred Dunhill Links Championship and a Palmer Cup at Royal County Down, birdied the first four holes and then played the remaining 14 in level par despite a double-bogey at the 15th. Haydn Porteous, winner of the Joburg Open at the start of the year, eagled both the fourth and sixth holes before birdieing the seventh and the eighth to be out in 30, the best of the day. At six-under-par the 22-year-old

Steve Stricker only made a par-five at the sixth hole but came home in 33 for a 67.

New starter David Lancaster greets Luke Donald on the first tee.

South African was leading The Open. Alas, in keeping with Reed's prediction, he came home in 40 strokes.

A total of 50 players scored under par for the day, but the start to the inward half wrecked more than a few cards. Worst of all there were nines for David Duval, Steven Bowditch and Kristoffer Broberg at the fearsome Railway hole, the 11th. Overall for the day, the second nine played almost two strokes over its par, while the first nine was not far off a stroke under it.

Only 26 players broke par coming home, and it showed how the wind dropped in the afternoon that only eight of those came in the morning, with 33s for Stricker, Horschel and Justin Rose, who was tucked in among those on 68. Louis Oosthuizen's inward 34, for a 71, was aided by the 2010 Champion Golfer of the Year holing a six-iron for an ace at the 178-yard par-three 14th.

Miguel Angel Jiménez, an afternoon starter, which may or may not explain the ageless Spaniard's 40

Despite a bogey on 15, Andy Sullivan returned a 67.

Winning the battle within

An opening 67, including birdies at the eighth and the 18th holes, was not only Søren Kjeldsen's lowest round in a previously undistinguished Open career but a good memory to set against some traumatic experiences.

In particular, at Royal Birkdale in 2008, in heavy rain and strong winds, the Dane opened with an 81. "I'll never forget walking off the 18th and there was one guy from Danish media," Kjeldsen explained. "You could see he was all dry. He had just had a nice cup of coffee, I could smell it on his breath. I had just shot 11-over-par and thought I didn't do too bad. It was crazy. His first question was, 'What happened out there?' I think I said, 'Maybe you should try and walk outside the tent.'"

Kjeldsen, never the longest off the tee but always a tidy performer in a steady European Tour career, struggled for form and desire as he turned 40, but victory in the Irish Open at Royal County Down in 2015 and finishing seventh at the 2016 Masters helped him realise he simply had to stick to his own game. "I found it really hard for a couple of years and you have certainly heard the story before when people get to 40 and it is all downhill from there," he said.

"But now I don't feel intimidated by anyone. I think I won the battle within. The media likes to say all the young guys are winning and you need to hit it 340 yards through the air, but I don't get caught up in that. I'm 41, I hit it 280 and try to make the most of it."

Although Mickelson strayed from the fairway at times, his recovery game was at its brilliant best.

Justin Thomas got into trouble at the 15th and took a six but still returned an opening 67.

Dream start for Gregory

Amateur champion Scott Gregory made a dream start to The 145th Open when he briefly found the top of the leaderboard at four-under-par. Playing alongside two former Champion Golfers of the Year in Sandy Lyle and David Duval, Gregory made a three at the first and added further birdies at the fourth, the sixth and the 10th holes.

And then he woke up. A triple-bogey seven at the 11th led to an inward 45 and an overall round of 78. Had he been startled by leading The Open? "Not really, I was just trying to get to five-under," he said. "I did watch the leaderboard as I like to know where I am. I felt completely comfortable, but unfortunately it went the other way."

The first Hampshire-born golfer to win The Amateur Championship added: "Hopefully at some point in my career I'll be leading at the 72nd hole and not the 10th. I've learnt a lot this week and chatting to Sandy was great."

Gregory, 21, beat Robert MacIntyre 2&1 in the final at Royal Porthcawl and is also exempt for the Masters and the US Open next year. He recovered with a 73 on the Friday but missed the cut along with the only other amateur in the field, Italy's Stefano Mazzoli, the European Amateur champion.

The pair would face each other the following week at the St Andrews Trophy between Great Britain and Ireland and the Continent of Europe at Prince's. The match was tied, so the home team retained the trophy.

to the turn, matched Mickelson's back nine of 31 for the best of the day, helped by chipping in for an eagle at the 16th. Mickelson's game was so strong that, by his standards, there was no need for anything too extravagant and he never looked like dropping a shot.

His start was the model of consistency: par, birdie, repeat. His gains came at the second, the fourth, the sixth and the eighth, where he spun his tee shot back close to the hole, plus the 10th. The sequence failed, though with nothing worse than a par, at the 12th. It was a hole he struggled on all week, his recovery sklls required to their fullest at times.

Being left-handed, Mickelson explained, meant the terrors of the back nine were not as severe for him. "I actually feel a bit more comfortable on the back nine than I do on the front," he said. "The golf course plays differently for me than the right-handed players. Going out it's a slice wind for me and I am a bit more cautious on the birdie holes. I feel I can take advantage on the back nine when it is a hook wind for me."

He picked up his second birdie coming home at the short 14th thanks to a putt of 25 feet. He then birdied the 16th and only then realised that if he birdied the final two holes a 62 could be his. "The problem is 17 is such a hard hole," he said. "It is one of the hardest par threes I've played and I was not thinking two."

But then Mickelson hit his best shot of the day, a four-iron to 15 feet. "It was perfectly struck," he said. "It soared through the air on a straight line, just staying left of the pin, which is where I needed it, and it gave me an opportunity. It gave me a putt. When the putt went in, I knew I had a chance."

He just missed a bunker on the left of the 18th fairway with his three-wood off the tee which he "held on to a little" due to the magnitude of the

Rickie Fowler tees off at the par-three fifth hole.

Keegan Bradley, who went on to score a 67, just misses his birdie-putt at the eighth hole.

Zach Johnson began the defence of his title with a 67.

occasion — as he explained to Ernie Els, his playing partner, when Ernie checked that Phil knew a 62 was on the cards walking up the fairway. There was nothing wrong with the six-iron he hit from the semi-rough to 18 feet, pin high. At the green, he told Bones, his caddie: "I need the best read of your life. I don't know if you know this..." Bones was fully aware of the situation. "Oh, I know..."

Mickelson recalled: "The line was a few inches outside the hole, breaking left in the middle, then straight the last bit. Well, it was supposed to be straight the last bit."

"I don't know how that putt didn't go in," Els said. "That would have been something. He played beautifully. The way he played out there today, it's amazing he has only won one Open." The third member of the group, Lee Westwood, had played alongside each of the first two Major winners of the year, Danny Willett at the Masters and Dustin Johnson at the US Open. His presence

Mickelson birdied the 16th from sand but was not yet thinking of a 62.

was not quite enough to help Mickelson make history this time.

From the swiftness of the Oakmont greens, where Johnson won his first Major title the previous month, to the relatively slow surfaces of Troon, running under 10 on the Stimpmeter, the US Open champion struggled with his putting in a 71. But his playing partner Kaymer compiled a tidy 66 in which he did not drop a stroke and collected three birdies in a row at the sixth, seventh and eighth holes.

Earlier, Bubba Watson had stumbled with a triple-bogey at the Postage Stamp when he found the Coffin bunker and had to play out sideways. Willett had a 71 playing in his first Open as a Major Champion, the same score as Jordan Spieth, whose game was summed up when he received the novel enquiry, for him, of what was wrong with his putting.

Round of the Day: Phil Mickelson – 63

OFFICIAL SCORECARD
THE 145TH OPEN
ROYAL TROON

Phil MICKELSON
Game 37
Thursday 14 July at 1:26pm

		FOR R&A USE ONLY		ROUND 1 18 HOLE TOTAL
		THIS ROUND	63	63
		VERIFIED		

ROUND 1

Hole	1	2	3	4	5	6	7	8	9	Out	10	11	12	13	14	15	16	17	18	In	Total
Yards	367	390	377	555	209	601	401	123	422	3445	451	482	430	473	178	499	554	220	458	3745	7190
Par	4	4	4	5	3	5	4	3	4	36	4	4	4	3	4	5	5	3	4	35	71
Score	4	3	4	4	3	4	4	2	4	32	3	4	4	4	2	4	4	2	4	31	63

Signature of Marker

Signature of Competitor
Phil Mickelson

FIRST ROUND LEADERS

	HOLE	1	2	3	4	5	6	7	8	9	10	11	12	13	14	15	16	17	18	
	PAR	4	4	4	5	3	5	4	3	4	4	4	4	4	3	4	5	3	4	TOTAL
Phil Mickelson		4	3	4	4	3	4	4	2	4	3	4	4	4	2	4	4	2	4	63
Patrick Reed		4	4	2	4	3	4	3	3	4	5	4	3	5	3	4	5	3	3	66
Martin Kaymer		4	4	4	5	3	4	3	2	4	4	4	4	3	4	4	3	4	4	66
Justin Thomas		3	3	3	4	3	5	3	3	4	5	4	4	3	3	6	5	3	3	67
Steve Stricker		4	5	4	4	2	5	4	3	3	5	4	4	4	2	4	4	3	3	67
Billy Horschel		4	4	5	5	2	4	4	2	4	4	4	4	3	3	4	5	2	4	67
Tony Finau		4	4	4	4	2	5	4	3	4	4	4	4	3	3	4	5	3	3	67
Søren Kjeldsen		4	3	4	4	4	4	4	2	4	4	4	5	3	4	4	3	3	3	67
Andy Sullivan		4	3	4	4	4	6	3	2	4	4	4	3	4	3	5	4	3	3	67
Zach Johnson		3	3	4	4	3	5	4	2	4	4	4	4	4	2	4	4	4	5	67
Keegan Bradley		4	3	4	4	3	4	3	4	4	4	4	5	3	3	4	3	4	4	67

▦ EAGLE OR BETTER ▦ BIRDIES ▦ BOGEYS ▦ DBL BOGEYS/WORSE

SCORING SUMMARY

FIRST ROUND SCORES

Players Under Par	50
Players At Par	24
Players Over Par	81

LOW SCORES

Low First Nine
Haydn Porteous	30

Low Second Nine
Phil Mickelson	31
Miguel Angel Jiménez	31

Low Round
Phil Mickelson	63

FIRST ROUND HOLE SUMMARY

HOLE	PAR	YARDS	EAGLES	BIRDIES	PARS	BOGEYS	D.BOGEYS	OTHER	RANK	AVERAGE
1	4	367	0	31	113	11	1	0	15	3.885
2	4	390	0	26	100	26	4	0	9	4.051
3	4	377	1	30	111	13	1	0	13	3.891
4	5	555	3	73	64	13	3	0	18	4.615
5	3	209	0	19	111	26	0	0	10	3.045
6	5	601	5	51	82	16	2	0	17	4.737
7	4	401	0	39	96	20	1	0	13	3.891
8	3	123	0	33	91	25	4	3	8	3.064
9	4	422	0	30	103	18	4	1	11	3.994
OUT	**36**	**3,445**	**9**	**332**	**871**	**168**	**20**	**4**		**35.173**
10	4	451	0	8	99	41	6	2	2	4.333
11	4	482	0	6	80	45	11	14	1	4.705
12	4	430	0	15	110	28	3	0	6	4.122
13	4	473	0	9	105	34	6	1	4	4.258
14	3	178	1	32	93	27	2	0	12	2.981
15	4	499	0	12	93	40	8	2	3	4.323
16	5	554	4	42	91	13	4	1	16	4.832
17	3	220	0	12	102	33	7	1	5	3.245
18	4	458	0	23	100	30	2	0	7	4.071
IN	**35**	**3,745**	**5**	**159**	**873**	**291**	**49**	**21**		**36.871**
TOTAL	**71**	**7,190**	**14**	**491**	**1,744**	**459**	**69**	**25**		**72.026**

A lot better players than me in the world of golf would have taken 71 after being two-over at the first. So, I'm proud of myself for hanging on because it would have been easy, very easy, to score 78 from there.
—Colin Montgomerie

It's The Open Championship, and you know coming in here you're going to have to battle the elements somewhat.
—Rory McIlroy

Just frustrating. It could have been a really good day but it ended up just being average. It would have been nice to post a decent number.
—Danny Willett

It was just one of those yucky days.
—Sandy Lyle

The 11th hole is one of the toughest holes I've ever played. It's a scary tee shot. You just can't see where you're going.
—Billy Horschel

If I'm patient and I just start hitting the correct shots and give myself the opportunities, I can get myself back in the tournament.
—Jason Day

This is the first time I've played links golf. I grew up watching it on TV, so I thought I could get a bit of a sense of it, but it's a lot different when you finally get here.
—Tony Finau

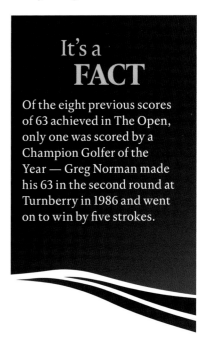

It was holing from 15 feet on the 17th for his eighth birdie that put Mickelson within reach of history.

World No 1 Jason Day struggled with his long game in a 73. Rory McIlroy, having missed the chance to defend his title from Royal Liverpool when he was injured playing football in 2015, appeared to be sailing along at four-under-par before flushing a six-iron over the green at the 13th and taking a double-bogey. Annoyed with himself, he also dropped a stroke at the next before finishing with a 69.

Zach Johnson was also enjoying playing for the first time in The Open as Champion Golfer of the Year. The winner from last time at St Andrews was lying in second place before bogeys at the last two holes dropped him back to four-under-par.

Alongside Johnson was Stenson, whose highlights included an eagle at the sixth plus birdies at the 12th, 14th and 16th holes. Despite bogeys at the 11th and 13th, the Swede was quietly under par for the inward half — as he would be each day that followed.

For now, though, Mickelson held centre stage. The putt-that-would-not-drop had robbed him of a 62, but would it also deny him a second Claret Jug?

It's a
FACT

Of the eight previous scores of 63 achieved in The Open, only one was scored by a Champion Golfer of the Year — Greg Norman made his 63 in the second round at Turnberry in 1986 and went on to win by five strokes.

Mickelson hit by the curse of 62

Peter Dixon says the American is not the first to fall foul of the golfing gods

There but for the golfing gods — the curse of 62 strikes again to Mickelson's horror (top right).

When Phil Mickelson was asked why he thought there had been 28 scores of 63 in the Major Championships but none of 62, he wasted little time in considering an answer. It was obvious, he said, "There's a curse."

Mickelson had just come within a lip-out of the magical, mythical 62 in the first round of The 145th Open at Royal Troon and was feeling a little sore.

At that point he was leading the field by three strokes, after a magnificent eight-under-par round of 63, and yet he felt the gods were toying with him, using him for their sport.

"If there wasn't a curse that ball would have been in and I would have had that 62," he lamented.

So he believed in the golfing gods, then? "I didn't, but I do now," he replied, mostly in jest.

A player with a keen sense of history and an awareness of his place in the game, Mickelson, at 46, knew only too well that such chances are few and far between. It was 43 years since Johnny Miller became the first player to card a 63 in Major Championships — at the 1973 US Open at Oakmont — and what his fellow American would have given to become the first player to better it.

"I hit a good putt on the right line with the right speed and, unfortunately, the curse hit me hard," Mickelson said of his 18-foot putt at the last.

"This one's going to stay with me for a while because of the historical element of Major Championships. The opportunity to shoot 62, and be the first one to do it, I just don't think that's going to come around again. And that's why I walked away so disappointed.

"There's lots of guys that have shot 63 but nobody has shot 62. That would have been really special. So to have that putt lip out, that's going to sting for a while."

It is hard not to believe that once the barrier is broken, others will drive on through. But it is extraordinary to think that none of the greats of the game have been able to break 63 in the Majors.

A few, like Mickelson, have come agonisingly close. Take Nick Price, for example. The 1994 Champion Golfer of the Year had a 30-foot putt for a 62 during the third round of the Masters in 1986. Like Mickelson at Royal Troon, the Zimbabwean thought his ball was in, only for it to do a full circle of the hole before choosing not to drop. "Bobby Jones' hand came up and popped it out," Price said.

The best chance to break 63 at The Open fell to Greg Norman in the second round at Turnberry in 1986. The Australian needed two putts from around 28 feet for a 62, but was thinking primarily of sinking his putt for a birdie and a round of 61. He ran his first putt five feet past the hole and missed the one coming back. "I didn't think about my score on the second putt, I just missed it," he said.

If that was surprising, given the way Norman had putted on the previous 17 holes, what is to be made of Jack Nicklaus' miss from three feet at the US Open at Baltusrol in 1980?

In such circumstances, most people would have bet their lives on the most successful player the game has known setting a new record. His explanation? "I just totally choked," he says.

Even Tiger Woods has suffered at the fickle hand of fate. The winner of 14 Major Championships, including The Open three times, the American thought he had bagged a 62 at the 2007 PGA Championship at Southern Hills when his putt from 15 feet went half way down the hole before popping back up again in defiance of gravity. "That would have been a nice little record to have," Woods said. Indeed it would.

Interestingly, the second 63 of the week at Troon came in the final round in what turned out to be a head-to-head challenge between Mickelson and Henrik Stenson, the eventual winner. To be fair, Stenson would not have been thinking of the record when he held the Claret Jug aloft on the final green. In a quieter moment, however, the Swede may well reflect on what might have been had he not opened his round with a bogey on one of the most straightforward holes on the course.

Tom Weiskopf, winner of The Open at Troon in 1973 and himself a member of the '63 Club,' says of the elusive 62: "It's like the four-minute mile." That, too, was a record that was hard to break until Roger Bannister stepped forward at Iffley Road, Oxford, in 1954.

Who, one wonders, is to be golf's Roger Bannister? It's in the lap of the gods.

SECOND ROUND

15 July 2016

Survival of the Fittest

By Andy Farrell

With Troon's South Beach running hard to the right of the first couple of fairways, here is seaside golf at its finest. And one of the glories of the British seaside is the changeable nature of the weather, from morning to afternoon, from hour to hour.

Inevitably when competing in The Open, where play lasts almost from dawn to dusk, there is the "luck of the draw" with which to contend. The players know it, and may even think it is part of the charm, but dealing with it is another matter.

How much energy is consumed by studying the forecasts, anticipating who will be aided, and who hindered, by the elements? It is an understandable yet futile pursuit. On a gloriously sunny day like Thursday, being off early might be favoured as surely the wind will only increase through the afternoon. But no, it dropped away.

Thursday afternoon's starters were out again

A birdie from sand at the 16th helped Henrik Stenson to a 65.

on Friday morning with a forecast for rain. It was heavy when it arrived, but they were into the round by then and did not have to deal with the gales of the afternoon. As so often, rather than evening itself out over the two days, one half of the draw fared better than the other.

But there is good fortune and there is taking advantage of it. To succeed in The Open, it helps to throw out the preconceived notions and adapt to situations as they arrive. Take Henrik Stenson. The Swede returned a 65 that was every bit as good as Phil Mickelson's 63 from the day before, better perhaps given the day's scoring average was over two strokes higher than in the first round.

"We were expecting a downpour when you pulled the curtain up in the morning, and it wasn't," Stenson said of the dank, overcast but rain-free start to the day. "You always felt it was going to start at some point, but it was nice to get the warm-up out of the way.

"It was quite playable the first five holes and I managed to take advantage and birdie three of them before the rain hit." In fact he made three birdies in a row from the third, an exquisite long bunker shot aiding the four at the par-five fourth.

Stenson took advantage of the calm conditions early on before "the fun really started" later on.

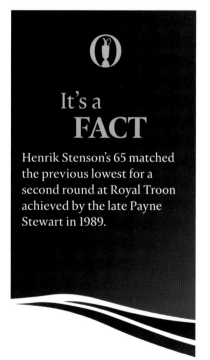

It's a
FACT

Henrik Stenson's 65 matched the previous lowest for a second round at Royal Troon achieved by the late Payne Stewart in 1989.

"Then it eased off and I birdied another one at the seventh. So my timing was good throughout the front nine. The only bogey was a bit of a soft one, a bit clumsy — I missed the second shot right on nine and didn't get up and down.

"Then the fun really started. It was blowing a bit more and starting to rain quite heavily, and I birdied 10 in those conditions." In the worst conditions of the day so far, Stenson hit an eight-iron to five feet to restore the shot he had dropped at the previous hole. "It started to get a bit nasty there and I was running out from under the umbrella to hit the shot, definitely a good one given the circumstances.

"Then I was hanging on for dear life on 11 and 12. They were playing tough and I got away with a couple of pars. Then I finished up quite tidily with another couple of birdies on the way home."

This last was said with typical Stensonian understatement. His inward 32 was not matched, let alone beaten, all day. As the rain

Phil Mickelson maintained his lead with a 69 on Friday.

Jordan Spieth watches his drive on the second sail away on the wind during his 75.

Stenson finishes tidily at the 18th.

continued he did not make a bogey on the way home and collected a three at the 13th and, thanks to another fine bunker shot at a par-five, a four at the 16th.

At nine-under-par, Stenson was now just one behind Mickelson, who remained at the top of the leaderboard after a second round of 69. The American, three ahead of the field overnight, had at first looked to be opening up a substantial advantage, but the quality of Stenson's performance — no one could match his tally of 31 greens

Round of the Day: Henrik Stenson – 65

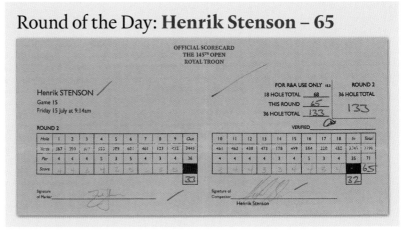

Padraig Harrington keeps an eye on his pitch at the last but bogeyed for a 72.

found in regulation for the first two rounds — had kept the Swede within touching distance of the American.

"I was five back of Phil from yesterday," Stenson said, "so, of course, I was hoping to gain a little, and the way it turned out I gained quite a lot. It's still early in the tournament though. We are only halfway through, or not even there. But I am happy with the way I played. It's not easy out there."

It was only going to get harder, but at Friday lunchtime it was not yet clear that Mickelson and Stenson would end the day first and second on the leaderboard. But it looked likely. At 40 years old, with a number of near-misses in Majors, including his runner-up finish to Mickelson in The Open in 2013, Stenson had a sense of urgency to win one of golf's biggest titles. "I'm not going to play these tournaments for ever and ever," he said. "I don't have another 50 goes at them, it might be a dozen or 15. If I keep putting myself in position and knocking on the door, I hope I get a couple of good breaks at the right times. But after six Majors of not being in contention, it's certainly time to get going."

Mickelson, also relishing the conditions despite having grown up in southern California where golf was avoided on the rare days like these, had shown no signs of slowing down from his explosive start on Thursday. At the second green, his par-putt toppled into the hole when it might not otherwise have done so. It maintained his momentum of not having dropped a shot, but what gold he would have given up for his putt for 62 at the 18th on Thursday

"There were two spectacular meltdowns in Troon during The Open Championship's second round. The first was when an overhead camera at the practice range burst into flames, the second when Rory McIlroy reached the turn and coughed up four bogeys in the space of five holes."
—Alasdair Read, *The Times*

"Using a metal clip to inelegantly tighten his cap so it wouldn't blow away, Mickelson plotted his way around the course with all the maturity of a 46-year-old seeking to become the second oldest winner of the Claret Jug."
—Philip Reid, *The Irish Times*

"Sharp and amusing in his interactions, Stenson did not look like a man struggling to cope with the fact that he could be in contention for his first Open victory come tomorrow evening."
—Moira Gordon, *The Scotsman*

"How is it, given the number of high-class performers that Sweden in particular, but the region as a whole has produced over the past 30 years, that it has still not produced a male winner of a Major Championship?"
—Kevin Ferrie, *The Herald*

Mickelson taps in at the Postage Stamp after almost making an ace.

to have done the same rather than spinning out.

There appeared little reaction for the 46-year-old from his disappointment of the night before and he quickly birdied the fourth and then the seventh before almost holing in one at the eighth. A second two in as many days at the Postage Stamp put Mickelson at 11-under-par and leading The Open by five strokes.

He eventually dropped a stroke at the 12th, having gone bogey-free for the first 29 holes, and though he claimed a two at the 14th, he leaked another shot at the 15th. Another bogey would have arrived at the 17th but for a moment of short-game brilliance. Having pulled his tee shot into a bunker on the right of the green, the left-hander found himself battling an awkward stance, playing to a hole on the left of the green.

"Because the sand was wet, it usually comes out a little faster, so it made the shot easier for such a long bunker shot," he explained. "But I didn't have the best stance, it was a little tight. I had to aim fractionally more to the right of the hole than I wanted to and opened up the face to offset that. I hit it up there close and got it up and down. That was a big momentum keeper."

Sergio Garcia and caddie Glen Murray braving the elements.

Rickie Fowler, one-under-par, and Jason Day, one-over-par, smiling in the face of meteorological adversity.

His halfway total of 132 was a new record in The Open at Royal Troon, beating the 133 of Bobby Clampett in 1982 and Darren Clarke in 1997. As he had not won anywhere in the three years since he claimed the Claret Jug at Muirfield, Mickelson was savouring all aspects of the situation. "I really enjoy the challenge that this weather and these elements provide," he said.

"I thought it was a good round to back up the low round yesterday. I played almost stress-free golf again. For the most part I kept the ball in play, only made one or two bad swings that led to bogeys. One of the things I've really worked on over the years is getting the ball onto the ground off the tee quickly. That two-iron I hit gives a low

Charl Schwartzel birdied four of the first five holes.

US Open champion Dustin Johnson had a 69.

Mickelson drives at the 10th on a day when even the planes at Prestwick Airport struggled to line up with their target.

shot that does that, so the ground is affecting the ball more than the air."

Avoiding disasters was not easy, as Ben Curtis unwittingly showed at the third. The 2003 Champion Golfer of the Year took a 10 after hitting six bunker shots from three different traps. But Denmark's Søren Kjeldsen got round without dropping a stroke, an achievement only Marc Leishman could match, in a 68. A two at the 17th was the highlight of his round, and with Stenson also on the charge, as one newspaper put it, it was "Norses for courses."

Kjeldsen finished at seven-under-par alongside Keegan Bradley, who also had a 68. Bradley, the 2011 PGA champion, had struggled for form of late, but this was not the first time he had appeared on the leaderboard during the week. During a practice round late on Monday afternoon, the American had climbed up to the traditional scoreboard on the 18th grandstand and spelled out his own

A sudden squall knocked Jamie Donaldson off balance.

Prayers for Nice

For Frenchman Clément Sordet the Friday of The 145th Open was a day of deep sadness — not for trifling golfing reasons but for what had taken place the night before in his home city of Nice.

Sordet had woken to news of the Bastille Day attack in which 85 men, women and children died after a lorry ploughed into crowds celebrating France's national day.

Understandably, the 23-year-old French player's first thought was for his girlfriend Marie and her family and friends, who were back home in Nice. They were all safe, but as he turned his focus to playing golf, being in the first group out at 6.35am, he wanted to pay his own tribute to the victims.

Sordet teed-off with "Pray for Nice" written on his cap, while all players in the field wore black ribbons in memory of those who had died. Above the 18th grandstand, the French Tricolore was flown at half-mast.

"I woke up at four in the morning as I had an early tee time and I knew straight away [what had happened] as I had texts from people asking if I was okay," Sordet said. "It happened maybe 500 metres from where I live, really close to the beach.

"I tried not to think about it, which is why I had this on my hat, and I tried just to enjoy my last day at The Open." In the event a second 75 was almost an irrelevance. He missed the cut, but there were far bigger things to worry about. "We all need to support each other," he added.

Steve Stricker had 17 pars but an eight at the 15th.

name. "It's so cool seeing your name up there," he said. "We climbed up there, though I probably shouldn't have said that."

Zach Johnson continued a fine defence of his title to be five-under-par, but was hampered again by a poor finish, playing the last four in two-over-par. At four-under-par were Tony Finau, Bill Haas, Charl Schwartzel, Sergio Garcia and Andrew Johnston. Rapidly becoming a cult hero, Johnston was having a whale of a time and enjoying the elongated cries of "Beef" — his nickname, a long story — from the gallery. His 69 would have been even better but for a seven at the 11th after he shanked onto the railway line. "I was like, where did that come from?" he said. "But then after that I was flushing it, didn't miss a shot."

It took a word from a friend for Schwartzel to find the key to playing in bad weather, and it worked as he birdied four of the first five holes. The South African went out in 31, the best of the day, and returned a 66.

Rory McIlroy birdied the sixth hole but later had four bogeys in five holes in a 71.

Keegan Bradley tied for third place after a 68.

Marc Leishman did not drop a shot in a 69.

Andrew "Beef" Johnston, tied sixth, a new fan favourite.

His friend? None other than the Champion Golfer of the Year in 2010, Louis Oosthuizen. "He kept telling me, 'Hit it softer. Hit it softer. You're hitting it too hard.' Today's probably the best I have played in these sorts of conditions because I kept my tempo and was able to control the ball flight and distance well." It was even more remarkable since Schwartzel had switched equipment companies at the start of the week and was playing with a completely new set of clubs.

All of those in the top 14 after two rounds — including Martin Kaymer, who was lying second overnight and added a 73 — had come from the late-early half of the draw. Only Patrick Reed, after a 74, Byeong Hun An, after a 70, and Rory McIlroy, after a 71, were in the top 21 from those

Martin Kaymer was three-under-par after a 73.

Inspiring Southgate makes the weekend

Battling to make the cut for the first time in The Open, Matthew Southgate parred the entire back nine until he birdied the last for a second successive 71. Then he watched as the qualifying mark for the weekend rose to four-over-par.

"I couldn't believe it," said the 27-year-old from Southend. "I was gobsmacked, watching the golf with my caddie and dad all afternoon, the cut just kept drifting. When I was on 18 I was thinking one-over might make it, but then again it might not. So when I sank that putt for birdie on 18 I thought, 'Yes, I've made it.' I gave it a real fist pump."

Southgate has been attending The Open since he was 10 — "My family loves The Open" — and has twice won at Final Qualifying, at Sunningdale in 2014 and at Royal Cinque Ports this year. He missed the cut at Royal Liverpool on his debut in 2014, and the following year was stuck at home watching on television after undergoing surgery for testicular cancer.

Remarkably, he returned to golf in time to go through three stages of the European Tour Qualifying School to earn his card for 2016 and was in tears as he claimed his best ever finish of fourth at the Irish Open. Here he was one of only three players to come through Final Qualifying and make the cut, along with Colin Montgomerie and Ryan Evans.

Though he has recovered, his niece Hattie still battles leukaemia, and the whole family is involved in initiatives such as getting people to join the bone marrow register. "If people have been inspired by my story, I'd really say, please think about joining," Southgate said. "It could mean so much to someone."

Patrick Reed battled his way to a 74.

Byeong Hun An impressed with a 70.

Zach Johnson stayed in contention with a 70.

Søren Kjeldsen's 68 put the Dane in third place.

Mickelson consults with caddie Jim "Bones" Mackay.

playing in the early-late half of the field.

"It's The Open and some draws go your way and some don't," McIlroy said. "The last Open I played, I got the good end of the draw and good things happened that week." Having missed The Open in 2015, he had, of course, won the prior year. "This year not so much, but I'm not going to let being on the wrong side ruin my mood or my week." Missing short putts at the ninth and 10th greens, however, might have done.

As the rain returned, poor Steve Stricker took an eight at the 15th, somewhat spoiling a card that otherwise contained 17 pars. Jason Day also played the 15th about then. "I couldn't get home. It was like a three-shot par-four," he said. His 70 was one of only four sub-par rounds from the afternoon starters. There had been 16 sub-par rounds from the morning.

All afternoon the cutline crept higher and higher. Colin Montgomerie finished at four-over-par in mid-afternoon and thought he had no chance. But inexorably the qualifying mark rose from two to three to four. Bubba Watson produced a magnificent birdie on the 18th to make it, while Jordan Spieth and Danny Willett holed good par putts to survive.

Sometimes that is all that can be hoped for at The Open. It is a case of survival of the fittest and, so far, it was Mickelson and Stenson who were adapting to their environment best of all.

SECOND ROUND LEADERS

HOLE	1	2	3	4	5	6	7	8	9	10	11	12	13	14	15	16	17	18	TOTAL
PAR	4	4	4	5	3	5	4	3	4	4	4	4	4	3	4	5	3	4	TOTAL
Phil Mickelson	4	4	4	4	3	5	3	2	4	4	4	5	4	2	5	5	3	4	69-132
Henrik Stenson	4	4	3	4	2	5	3	3	5	3	4	4	3	3	4	4	3	4	65-133
Søren Kjeldsen	4	4	4	4	3	4	4	3	4	4	4	4	4	3	4	5	2	4	68-135
Keegan Bradley	4	4	3	4	3	5	3	3	4	4	5	5	4	2	3	5	3	4	68-135
Zach Johnson	4	3	4	4	4	4	4	2	4	4	5	4	3	3	5	5	3	5	70-137
Tony Finau	4	4	5	4	3	5	5	3	5	4	4	3	4	4	4	5	2	4	71-138
Bill Haas	3	4	4	5	4	5	3	4	4	4	4	5	4	3	5	4	2	4	70-138
Charl Schwartzel	3	4	3	4	2	5	3	3	4	5	4	5	3	2	4	5	3	4	66-138
Andrew Johnston	5	5	3	4	2	5	4	2	4	4	7	4	4	3	3	4	2	4	69-138
Sergio Garcia	4	4	4	5	3	4	4	3	4	4	4	5	4	2	4	4	3	5	70-138

■ EAGLE OR BETTER   ■ BIRDIES   ■ BOGEYS   ■ DBL BOGEYS/WORSE

SCORING SUMMARY

SECOND ROUND SCORES

Players Under Par	20
Players At Par	12
Players Over Par	122

LOW SCORES

Low First Nine	Charl Schwartzel	31
Low Second Nine	Henrik Stenson	32
Low Round	Henrik Stenson	65

SECOND ROUND HOLE SUMMARY

HOLE	PAR	YARDS	EAGLES	BIRDIES	PARS	BOGEYS	D.BOGEYS	OTHER	RANK	AVERAGE
1	4	367	0	16	106	29	3	0	12	4.123
2	4	390	0	16	100	35	0	3	8	4.182
3	4	377	0	19	100	30	4	1	10	4.162
4	5	555	1	37	94	18	4	0	17	4.916
5	3	209	0	20	90	41	3	0	9	3.175
6	5	601	0	22	99	27	5	1	14	5.117
7	4	401	0	24	94	31	3	2	12	4.123
8	3	123	0	31	98	17	5	3	15	3.039
9	4	422	0	6	91	48	7	2	3	4.403
OUT	**36**	**3,445**	**1**	**191**	**872**	**276**	**34**	**12**		**37.240**
10	4	451	0	7	93	45	7	2	4	4.377
11	4	482	0	10	89	36	15	4	1	4.455
12	4	430	0	6	89	51	5	3	2	4.429
13	4	473	0	14	100	36	2	2	7	4.214
14	3	178	0	25	107	19	3	0	16	3.000
15	4	499	0	14	85	44	8	3	5	4.370
16	5	554	0	41	93	15	5	0	18	4.896
17	3	220	0	10	98	42	4	0	6	3.260
18	4	458	0	17	103	29	5	0	11	4.143
IN	**35**	**3,745**	**0**	**144**	**857**	**317**	**54**	**14**		**37.143**
TOTAL	**71**	**7,190**	**1**	**335**	**1,729**	**593**	**88**	**26**		**74.383**

How many at the Postage Stamp?

Art Spander on the "Wee Beastie" that is short but challenges the best

The adjacent bunker, the one on the left of the green that devoured Bubba Watson's first round, has its own Twitter account and, naturally, as with every penalising feature of a course in Scotland, a frightening label, "Coffin."

The hole, so tiny — at just 123 yards, the shortest of any used at The Open — so captivating, so maddening, is an expression of that well-known club motto, *Tam Arte Quam Marte*, which doesn't exactly translate as "a smooth seven-iron to the green is worth more than a 300-yard drive into the gorse," but means the same.

We are referring, of course, to the par-three eighth at Royal Troon, the Postage Stamp, a name coined by William Park — no relation of The Open-winning Willie Park, Sr or Jr — who wrote in 1922, perhaps in elation but more likely irritation, that the green was the size of a postage stamp. Truth tell, according to Golfbidder, it would take 81,290 postage stamps, air or surface mail, to cover the green, which is 12 yards wide at the front and only 10 at the back.

But the idea is understood: If you don't land on the green, you're in trouble.

In the second round of The 145th Open, that windy, rainy Friday, Phil Mickelson's wedge shot not only was on the green but nearly in the hole, stopping inches short of a hole-in-one. "I just needed a little more sauce on it," Mickelson said, "and it would have gone in." He still recorded his second birdie in two rounds, his own cancellation on the Postage Stamp.

Short golf holes — the Postage Stamp, the 106-yard seventh at Pebble Beach, the 143-yard 15th at Cypress Point — are both a delight and a scourge. They give everyone, pro, high handicapper, a chance. A chance, that is, to make par or, because invariably the green is embraced by hazards, bunkers, creeks, whatever, to make a bundle.

In 1973, Gene Sarazen, then 71, got an ace at the hole and landed a birdie the next day by holing out from a bunker. In 1997, by contrast, Tiger Woods triple-bogeyed it.

No aces this Open, but some triple-bogeys. One was by Watson, who was in the lead when he arrived at the tee on the morning of the first round with the best weather of the week. Watson's shot plopped into the Coffin, with its four-foot depth and steep sides. Bubba may be a magician on some shots — consider that beauty out of the trees on Augusta's 10th in the play-off for the 2012 Masters — but he knows there are times when the rabbit is not coming out of the hat or the ball out of the trap in normal fashion.

He aimed away from the green and did get the ball

Bubba Watson: "I've been in that bunker all week. I love the hole, but every time I play it, it's killing me."

up and over the edge, if into deep rough behind the green. Watson later would shake his head and sigh, "I've been in that bunker all week. I love the hole, but every time I play it, it's killing me."

The 2014 Champion Golfer of the Year Rory McIlroy had his troubles at the Stamp during Tuesday's practice round, so if it had an effect on his confidence at least there was no evidence on his official scorecard. McIlroy said he needed six swings to extricate himself from the bunker opposite the Coffin, and had a nine.

"The lip is basically vertical," McIlroy said. "The ball would roll back into the same spot in the sand."

Henrik Stenson didn't need to prove anything to himself or anyone. During one of his practice rounds he gave up using a club and simply kicked the ball out of the bunker onto the green.

It must have put him in the right mood. A few days later he won The Open.

Royal Troon is an unfussy collection of holes, other than the 11th, the Railway and the eighth. "I

think the only conversation piece sometimes," Troon historian Douglas McCreath told the *New York Times*, "is how many did you score at the Postage Stamp?"

In 1950, an amateur from Germany, Hermann Tissies, had a 15.

And thus does the eighth have another nickname, a proper Scottish one, "Wee Beastie."

Troon members, if not guests, know when to go after the Beastie and when discretion is the better part of their game, just picking up the ball and going on. Admittedly that is not acceptable or permissible in The Open.

"Even for members," one local said, "it's the easiest hole on the course and it also can be the hardest." That is the mark of a great hole, one on which anything is possible, and naturally on a links course, so much is determined by the weather.

"Challenging a player for his precision as opposed to solely length is a lost art," said Mickelson. "The Postage Stamp is a perfect example of how you can challenge the best players in the world."

THIRD ROUND
16 July 2016

And Then There Were Two

By Andy Farrell

This was no perfunctory hand-shake at the end of a game of golf. The eyes locked on each other's, speaking of mutual respect and admiration — "That was fun, let's do it again tomorrow," was the gist.

It had been an enthralling contest of an exceptionally high standard given another day of tricky conditions. If there was a slight difference to be detected in the bearing of the two men it was this:
• Henrik Stenson, having delivered two stunning blows late in the piece, had the demeanour of a challenger ready to take the crown. "You may have won five Majors already and I'm trying to get my first, but now you know what you are up against."
• Phil Mickelson, a Champion Golfer of the Year already, from Muirfield three years earlier when Stenson finished second, had the air of someone already plotting how to raise his game for the

Henrik Stenson and Phil Mickelson at the 18th.

next day, to haul himself up to the summit one more time. "Oh, believe me, I know…"

Mickelson had started the third round with a one-stroke lead, had gone behind, then regained the lead, went two in front with five holes to play and ended up one behind. It was only Saturday but Royal Troon's closing stretch had already produced plenty of drama.

At the 13th hole Mickelson rolled in a 25-footer to double his advantage, the first time either man had been more than one stroke ahead all day. But at each of the remaining par threes there were two-shot swings in favour of Stenson.

It was now that the Swede's famed ball-striking, honed after so many hours of due diligence under the supervision of coach Peter Cowen, showed itself as a precision weapon. A five-iron to four feet at the 14th brought him back level as Mickelson three-putted. The American had been the last man on the course not to have dropped a shot during the round, and he recovered the lead once more at the par-five 16th by getting down in a pitch and a putt for a four.

Then came the 17th. Mickelson missed the green on the left. "It was an awful swing, I lunged

After nearly finding a bush off the tee, Mickelson produced a typically audacious par at the 12th hole.

All smiles as Stenson opened with a birdie.

forward," he admitted. The hole was playing 207 yards into a cold wind, if that amounts to mitigating circumstances, although nothing could restrain Stenson from lasering a three-iron to 20 feet. It was another mighty strike, but the blow only landed with full force when he holed the putt for a birdie as Mickelson took four.

Thankfully a cameraman's click on Mickelson's backswing for his second shot at the 18th came to nought as both men saved par. As they headed for the recorder's hut, where Mickelson would sign for a 70 and Stenson a best-of-the-day-equalling 68, the American conceded: "Henrik, that was a pretty sporty birdie you just did on 17."

"It was a nice one," Stenson reflected. "It gave me that little edge going into tomorrow. I've always been of the thought it's better to be one ahead than one behind, because that means Phil's got to play better than I do tomorrow, or whoever I'm up against."

The pair were respectively six and five strokes ahead of the man in third place, Bill Haas, and even he was of the view that this was not going to be anything other than a duel between the top

Bill Haas holed out from a bunker for a two at the Postage Stamp.

"So inseparable have Phil Mickelson and Henrik Stenson become over the past 24 hours, it would not come as a surprise to learn they've got magnets in their pockets."

—Graeme Macpherson,
Sunday Herald

"Finau isn't from normal golfing stock. From Samoan heritage, the kid and his brother Gipper were introduced to the sport by their father in a bid to keep them out of gangland culture in Utah."

—Craig Swan, *Sunday Mail*

"Away from the course Mickelson could scarcely be more relaxed. He turned up on Friday night at Maharani, an Indian restaurant in the centre of Troon, to eat a dish of butter chicken and exchange pleasantries with fellow customers."

—Oliver Brown,
Sunday Telegraph

"As no pursuer emerged from the pack, it became clear to both players that this was going to be a duel to the finish."

—Andrew Longmore,
Sunday Times

After turning in one-under-par for the day, Stenson again excelled on the second nine.

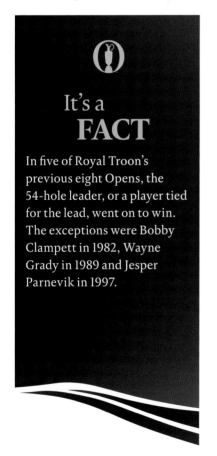

two. Mickelson, for his own reasons as he prepared for the final round of a Major rather than a private match, was having none of it. "No, not at all, no, I don't see that," he said.

Stenson, however, described how the closing stages of Saturday's round had felt. "It was certainly kind of a matchplay scenario out there. I was happy enough to throw two good punches in there on the par threes, pick up two shots on each and come out on top at the end of the third round. Because when Phil made the birdie on 13, he was in the driver's seat, and he made another good birdie on 16 when I had to make a good par save."

Stenson was at 12-under-par, setting a new 54-hole record for Troon Opens of 201, one lower than Jesper Parnevik's total at the same stage in 1997. Parnevik ended up finishing second in The Open for the second time in four years, a fate Stenson could do without, having finished second at Muirfield in 2013 and third twice, in 2008 and 2010.

"I know what I would like to see tomorrow, there's no question about it," said the Swede. "I've got a second and two thirds, so it's not like I'm looking to pick up any more of those finishes. There's only one thing that matters tomorrow. I know he's not going to back down and I'm certainly not going to back down either. So it should be an exciting afternoon."

On another windy day, R&A officials altered their early-morning set-up plans.

Asked if revenge was in the air from Muirfield, Stenson obliged headline writers. "There's always revenge," he smiled.

As yet this was no "Duel in the Sun," the Watson-Nicklaus barnstormer from down the coast at Turnberry in 1977 — at least meteorologically. Variations on the "Duel in the Drizzle/Rain/Wind" did not quite have the same zing. It was so cold when Stenson, wrapped up from head to toe, walked onto the practice range prior to the round that he squatted down as if over skis rather than about to participate in a summer sport.

The wind was still blowing at 15-20mph with gusts up to 30mph, so The R&A had decided not to cut or roll the greens and to keep them down to 9.5 on the Stimpmeter. A few pin positions were changed in the morning to accommodate the conditions and a few tees, the 11th, 15th and 16th holes among them, were moved up. The eighth hole, the Postage Stamp, measured only 100 yards and yet played harder than on any other day.

The adjustments, which ensured play was not delayed at any stage, were welcomed by the players. No one beat 68 all day, with the four players on that score spread throughout the draw, including Stenson in the last group and Haydn Porteous in the first. Playing with a marker, the club's head professional, Porteous actually came to the last on five-under-par for the day but ran his second shot

A bogey at the first hole set the tone for a frustrating day for Rory McIlroy.

A 72 left Dustin Johnson at one-under-par.

over the green and out of bounds in front of the clubhouse.

Steve Stricker was another to post a 68 and rose from 27th into a tie for sixth. "It felt like we played every hole into the wind or some sort of crosswind," said the 49-year-old. "You are grinding all the way round. It wears you out."

Among the strugglers were those close to the top two. In the penultimate pairing, both of whom started at seven-under-par, Søren Kjeldsen had a 75 to be three-under-par, and Keegan Bradley a 76. Zach Johnson, the defending Champion, had two double-bogeys in a 75 which saw his hopes of retaining the title frittered away on the wind.

Among those who prospered was JB Holmes, who matched Jason Day's 32 for the lowest outward nine. Playing on the weekend at The Open for the first time since 2010, the American had reached six-under-par at the turn, but bogeys at the 14th and 15th holes left him at four-under-par and in fifth place.

Fab Four playing out of tune

They arrived at Royal Troon as the "Fab Four" — world No 1 Jason Day, his predecessors Jordan Spieth (right) and Rory McIlroy, and new US Open champion Dustin Johnson — but by Saturday evening they were clearly only part of the supporting act to headliners Stenson and Mickelson.

Day and Spieth both narrowly missed the play-off at St Andrews the year before, but now languished at one-over-par and five-over-par respectively. Day had four birdies on the front nine but for the third day running could not make one on the inward half.

Both players came home in 39, Spieth's magical putting having been blown away on the wind. "I missed four putts inside of five feet," he said in a state of shock. "That's something that normally doesn't happen." The 22-year-old also revealed the pressure he felt at living up to his two Major wins of the previous season.

Johnson tangled with the gorse at the 11th and took a seven to surrender all the ground he had made up earlier in the round. He was one-under-par and one ahead of McIlroy, who never got going after missing short putts to bogey two of the first three holes.

Jordan Spieth

The Northern Irishman's frustrations boiled over at the 16th when he threw his three-wood to the ground so that the clubhead became detached from the shaft. "I'd let one go to the right on the previous hole and did the exact same thing again," he said. "No one likes to make the same mistake twice."

Though he saved par from a tricky spot on the 16th, Jason Day again struggled coming home.

Haydn Porteous posted the day's first 68.

Bunker trouble led to a six at the 15th for Sergio Garcia.

Kieron steps into the breach

As the head professional at Royal Troon, Kieron Stevenson spent most of the first two days of The Open working in the club shop. And then he was offered the never-to-be-forgotten chance to play in the final two rounds.

Stevenson received a call at 10pm on Friday asking him to play as a marker for Haydn Porteous in the third round because the halfway cut had left the field with an uneven number of players. The young South African was the first man out at 8.25am and Stevenson had the privilege of playing with him and marking his card.

This was a day Stevenson will never forget. "I knew I'd be playing if we had an odd number of players making the cut," he said. "I'd not been watching because I was busy in the shop. In fact I'll be in the shop this afternoon and back to normal.

"It was the most enjoyable round I've ever played. It was also the most nervous I've been on the first tee. I played all right but I didn't score because I didn't want to get in Haydn's way. I picked up a few times.

"We got round in good time and I think it worked in his favour being on his own. He played beautifully and was great to watch. The grandstands have been up for three months, so I've played a lot with them there. It was different, though, playing in front of people."

Porteous, who had a 68, was equally impressed. "Kieron's a really nice guy," he said. "We had a good laugh and he kept the round nice and light-hearted."

The next day was to prove equally good fun for Kieron. His playing partner? Colin Montgomerie — just another Sunday morning round with a Troon member.

Søren Kjeldsen's challenge faltered when his tee shot at the Postage Stamp ended in a bunker.

TV commentator David Feherty in traditional garb.

Andrew Johnston celebrates his chip-in at the 13th.

One stroke better placed was Andrew "Beef" Johnston. More than just a folk hero, the Londoner was showing some impressive ball-striking skills as he went out in 34 without dropping a shot. Johnston won the Spanish Open in April at a venue that requires a serious long game, Valderrama. No one appreciated that more than the event's host Sergio Garcia, who was playing alongside Johnston today.

There were a couple of dropped shots on the way home, but also one of the highlights of the entire week. Johnston's chip-in for a birdie at the 13th, and the reaction of the gallery, will live long in the memory.

There were three other hole-outs during the day. Justin Rose and Nicolas Colsaerts had two of them and Haas the other. Having found the bunker at the front of the eighth green — so many spun back into it, although Tony Finau was the unluckiest of all since his tee shot had hit the flagstick in passing — Haas claimed a dramatic two.

It put Haas at seven-under-par and it was the

JB Holmes moved up to fifth with a 69.

"This Falstaffian figure, with a beard that might have been hewn from extreme rough, has been England's best hope of success at Troon and his following gathers momentum with each hole."

— Paul Weaver, *The Observer*

"The Fab Four? Not so fab this week, alas, with McIlroy a mammoth 12 strokes off the lead and, like the other three, playing for pride."

—Derek Lawrenson, *Mail on Sunday*

"The 145th Open Championship has become a private party. The duel in the drizzle, 39 years on from those epic events down the coast at Turnberry."

—Ewan Murray, *The Observer*

"McIlroy has always had a love/hate relationship with links golf. He knew he had to play twist-or-bust golf as the gusts buffeted Troon. By the fifth hole he was bust."

—Paul Mahoney, *Sunday Express*

"It looks like a two-horse race over the closing 18 holes in The 145th Open Championship and ninth to be staged at Royal Troon."

—Martin Dempster, *Scotland on Sunday*

Mickelson plays his approach shot to the 18th.

Stenson birdied the 17th to lead by one.

closest anyone got to the runaway leaders. Haas promptly bogeyed the next but came home in level par for a 69. However, the 34-year-old American was realistic about his chances the following day. "You certainly can't expect Henrik Stenson and Phil Mickelson to fall backwards," he said. "I don't think they are feeling the pressure tonight sleeping knowing that Beef and Bill Haas are behind them."

If it was to be a battle of the "sons," Stenson and Mickelson were quite used to playing alongside each other in 2016. They were paired for the first two rounds of each of the Masters, the Players and the US Open. It had not gone particularly well. Only Stenson made the cut at the Masters, and at Oakmont the Swede withdrew in the second round with a knee injury.

Fortunately it had recovered sufficiently for the 40-year-old to win the BMW International Open in Germany the following week, an important boost that brought to an end a run of eight runner-up finishes since his last win in 2014. Stenson and Mickelson got back together for the third round of the Scottish Open at Castle Stuart the previous Saturday. Stenson scored a 66 that day,

Round of the Day: **Henrik Stenson – 68**

Henrik STENSON
Game 41
Saturday 16 July at 3:20pm

FOR R&A USE ONLY		ROUND 3
36 HOLE TOTAL	133	54 HOLE TOTAL
THIS ROUND	68	
54 HOLE TOTAL	201	201

VERIFIED

ROUND 3

Hole	1	2	3	4	5	6	7	8	9	Out	10	11	12	13	14	15	16	17	18	In	Total
Yards	367	390	377	555	209	601	401	123	422	3445	451	482	430	473	178	499	554	220	458	3745	7190
Par	4	4	4	5	3	5	4	3	4	36	4	4	4	4	3	4	5	3	4	35	71
Score	3	4	3	4	3	6	4	4	4	35	4	4	4	4	2	4	5	2	4	33	68

Signature of Marker

Signature of Competitor
Henrik Stenson

Mickelson the same a day later to set him up for his record-breaking start to The Open.

But it was Stenson who made the quickest start today, holing a 15-footer at the first and birdieing three of the first four holes. Mickelson could only match the three at the third, so Stenson led by one until three-putting at the sixth. A mis-hit tee shot at the eighth found a bunker, and a bogey put Mickelson ahead again.

Both were out in 35 but were in trouble on the turn for home. Mickelson's weak tee shots at the 11th and 12th holes had him scrambling to make pars. At the 12th his second shot was hampered by the gorse bush he had narrowly missed off the tee, but he conjured a typically brave up-and-down, spinning his pitch shot back down the slope at the back of the green. Stenson also required a chip and a putt to save par.

Though both men made two birdies over the last six holes, Mickelson could not keep saving himself forever. "Today was a day that could have got away from me," he said, "instead I shot under par and kept myself in it.

"I was off today," he added, noting that he had work to do with his coach Andrew Getson before the final round. "I tried to force it a little bit on the front nine and got out of rhythm. It was tough to get it back; I got a bit jumpy with my swing, but I found a way to make some pars like at 12. It's not too far off. Hopefully I'll get dialled back in tomorrow."

Of the whole field only Stenson had returned three scores under 70 and three sub-par inward nines. The Swede had not realised about the latter. "Thanks for reminding me, because I didn't have a clue," he said. "When I'm playing well, I'm

Mickelson recovered from a bunker to par the last.

> *Today could have been a day that got away from me, instead I shot under par and kept myself right in it.*
>
> —Phil Mickelson

> *I haven't won The Open just because I have the 54-hole lead. I'm just going to go out there and try my hardest. That's the only thing I can do.*
>
> —Henrik Stenson

> *I'm just really struggling on the greens this week. I've left everything short. I'm hitting the ball great but finding the putting very challenging.*
>
> —Jordan Spieth

> *It is probably the most unexpected cut I have made in my life. I was having a nap when my caddie phoned to say we were in.*
>
> —Graeme McDowell

> *It has just been a frustrating week, a grind start to finish.*
>
> —Danny Willett

> *The conditions are tough and poor ball-striking gets exposed when it's as windy as this.*
>
> —Lee Westwood

> *I could easily have been six or seven-under-par on the front side, but I haven't had a birdie on the back side all week and that's why I'm not in the tournament right now.*
>
> —Jason Day

> *They say this is summer but I'm not so sure.*
>
> —Patrick Reed

THIRD ROUND LEADERS

HOLE	1	2	3	4	5	6	7	8	9	10	11	12	13	14	15	16	17	18	TOTAL
PAR	4	4	4	5	3	5	4	3	4	4	4	4	4	3	4	5	3	4	TOTAL
Henrik Stenson	3	4	3	4	3	6	4	4	4	4	4	4	4	2	4	5	2	4	68-201
Phil Mickelson	4	4	3	5	3	5	4	3	4	4	4	4	3	4	4	4	4	4	70-202
Bill Haas	3	4	4	4	4	4	4	2	5	4	4	4	4	3	5	4	3	4	69-207
Andrew Johnston	4	4	4	5	3	5	3	3	5	4	4	4	3	4	4	5	3	4	70-208
JB Holmes	3	3	4	5	2	5	4	3	3	4	4	4	4	5	5	5	3	4	69-209

■ EAGLE OR BETTER ■ BIRDIES ■ BOGEYS ■ DBL BOGEYS/WORSE

SCORING SUMMARY

THIRD ROUND SCORES

Players Under Par	13
Players At Par	8
Players Over Par	60

LOW SCORES

Low First Nine

JB Holmes	32
Jason Day	32

Low Second Nine

Henrik Stenson	33

Low Round

Henrik Stenson	68
Steve Stricker	68
Haydn Porteous	68
Brandt Snedeker	68

THIRD ROUND HOLE SUMMARY

HOLE	PAR	YARDS	EAGLES	BIRDIES	PARS	BOGEYS	D.BOGEYS	OTHER	RANK	AVERAGE
1	4	367	0	13	60	7	1	0	14	3.951
2	4	390	0	9	55	14	3	0	9	4.136
3	4	377	0	19	53	8	1	0	15	3.889
4	5	555	0	33	42	5	1	0	18	4.679
5	3	209	0	8	49	21	3	0	6	3.235
6	5	601	1	21	49	8	2	0	16	4.864
7	4	401	0	17	50	13	1	0	13	3.975
8	3	123	0	10	51	18	0	2	7	3.173
9	4	422	0	14	53	13	1	0	12	4.012
OUT	36	3,445	1	144	462	107	13	2		35.914
10	4	451	0	2	36	34	8	1	2	4.630
11	4	482	0	4	49	18	5	5	3	4.519
12	4	430	0	6	59	15	1	0	9	4.136
13	4	473	0	5	49	26	1	0	4	4.284
14	3	178	0	9	60	12	0	0	11	3.037
15	4	499	0	2	34	37	7	1	1	4.642
16	5	554	0	25	47	7	2	0	17	4.827
17	3	220	0	6	60	13	2	0	8	3.136
18	4	458	0	5	57	15	2	2	5	4.247
IN	35	3,745	0	64	451	177	28	9		37.457
TOTAL	71	7,190	1	208	913	284	41	11		73.370

Stenson missed the green with his approach at the last but got up and down to secure a one-stroke lead after 54 holes.

pretty solid with the longer irons and there's a lot of long-irons coming in."

About facing Mickelson again the next day, Stenson said: "I enjoy his company. He's always fun to watch. He hits some spectacular shots and he's a great competitor. So it's inspiring. I know I'll have to bring my best. I would have had to bring my best no matter who I was out with tomorrow, but certainly when you are playing someone like Phil.

"I haven't won The Open just because I have the 54-hole lead. I will try my hardest, that's the only thing I can do," he added before ending with a lighthearted aside. "The sun will come up Monday anyway, hopefully. Maybe not in Scotland, but in other parts of the world."

Whatever the weather, we were down to two.

Brandt Snedeker and Steve Stricker also scored 68s.

Uncle Beef to the rescue

Alistair Tait witnesses The Open gallery adopt a new favourite

A new hero was born during The 145th Open. Step forward and take a bow Andrew "Beef" Johnston, the people's champion. The 27-year-old Englishman forged an alliance with golf fans at Royal Troon that had to be seen — and heard — to be believed.

Sergio Garcia doesn't often play second fiddle to anyone in The Open. He is one of Europe's most popular players, but Johnston fans vastly outnumbered Garcia supporters as the two played Troon's championship links in the third round.

Cries of "Beeeeef!" could be heard as the man from North London stepped onto the first tee at 2.40pm alongside Garcia. They increased in intensity as the round progressed.

Johnston's huge well of support derives from a physique that marks him out as more caddie than golfer. His ample frame points to a preference for a few beers after a round rather than a few crunches in the gym. He's also a bit of a rarity among tour players since he sports a fairly full beard. Then there's his nickname.

Johnston has answered to "Beef" ever since he started playing golf as a boy at North Middlesex Golf Club in North London. A friend looked at the mass of curly hair on his head and gave Johnston the moniker that has stuck ever since.

"My mate just went, 'Look at your hair. It's like a big bit of beef,' and called me a 'Beefhead.' That was it. It has been shortened to 'Beef.'"

It certainly resonated with the fans. Roars of "Beeeeef!" resounded on every hole.

"It's been amazing, man," Johnston said about the reception. "I absolutely love it. That's what it's about. A thousand people come and watch, and if they really enjoy themselves, that's what it's about. You want them to go home with good memories and go, 'Oh, my God, I've had such a great day.'"

Johnston gave his legion of fans a great Saturday. He really made their day at the 13th hole. Looking like he might drop a shot after missing the green, Johnston holed his chip shot to increase the roars of "Beeeeef!"

One member of the gallery couldn't contain her excitement.

"I walked over and I could see my mum crying, which was even funnier. And that got me going a bit. I was like, 'Oh my God. Don't look at mum.'"

Johnston first caught the attention in April when he won the Spanish Open. Asked how he was going to celebrate, he said he couldn't wait to get back to North Middlesex Golf Club and "get hammered" with his mates. That candidness went over well in a world where political correctness often stifles genuine character. It created a small battalion of Johnston supporters that grew into an army by the time he arrived at Troon. Among them was his five-year-old niece, Summer, who had her own special cries of "Uncle Beef" and "Beef to the rescue."

What you get from Andrew Johnston is exactly what you see. When he is not on tour he likes nothing more than to hang out with his friends, watch sport, preferably Arsenal FC, and have a few beers with his pals. Asked why he felt The Open galleries had taken to him so readily, Johnston was typically honest.

"I guess I'm just really down to earth," he said. "At the end of the day I'm just a normal guy who happens to play golf. I'm no different to anyone else. That's how I see it. I'll talk and chat to anyone. It really doesn't bother me. I like meeting new people and I don't care where they're from or who they are. If they're nice, I get on well with them and I'm going to make friends.

You've always got to remember where you've come from and where you've been. I always stay grounded. I'll always be the same person. That's the most important thing."

Johnston bettered Garcia by three shots, with a one-under-par 70 in wet conditions, to lie fourth when some felt he might fade under the pressure.

Not Johnston. He wasn't surprised at his lofty place on the leaderboard, or that he was playing in the penultimate pairing on Sunday.

"Why not? What's the point of playing if you don't believe or trust yourself?" he said.

This was some performance considering it was only his second appearance in The Open after missing the cut at Royal St George's in 2011. No wonder he was nervous as he stepped onto the first tee.

"If you don't have nerves, it doesn't mean that much to you. You've got to embrace those nerves. You've got to get outside yourself and go, 'No, no, come on, man, I'm playing well. Just keep doing what you're doing. Concentrate on what you're doing.' That's how I seem to deal with it."

He dealt with it extremely well in the third round at Royal Troon. He was 100 per cent grade-A Beef.

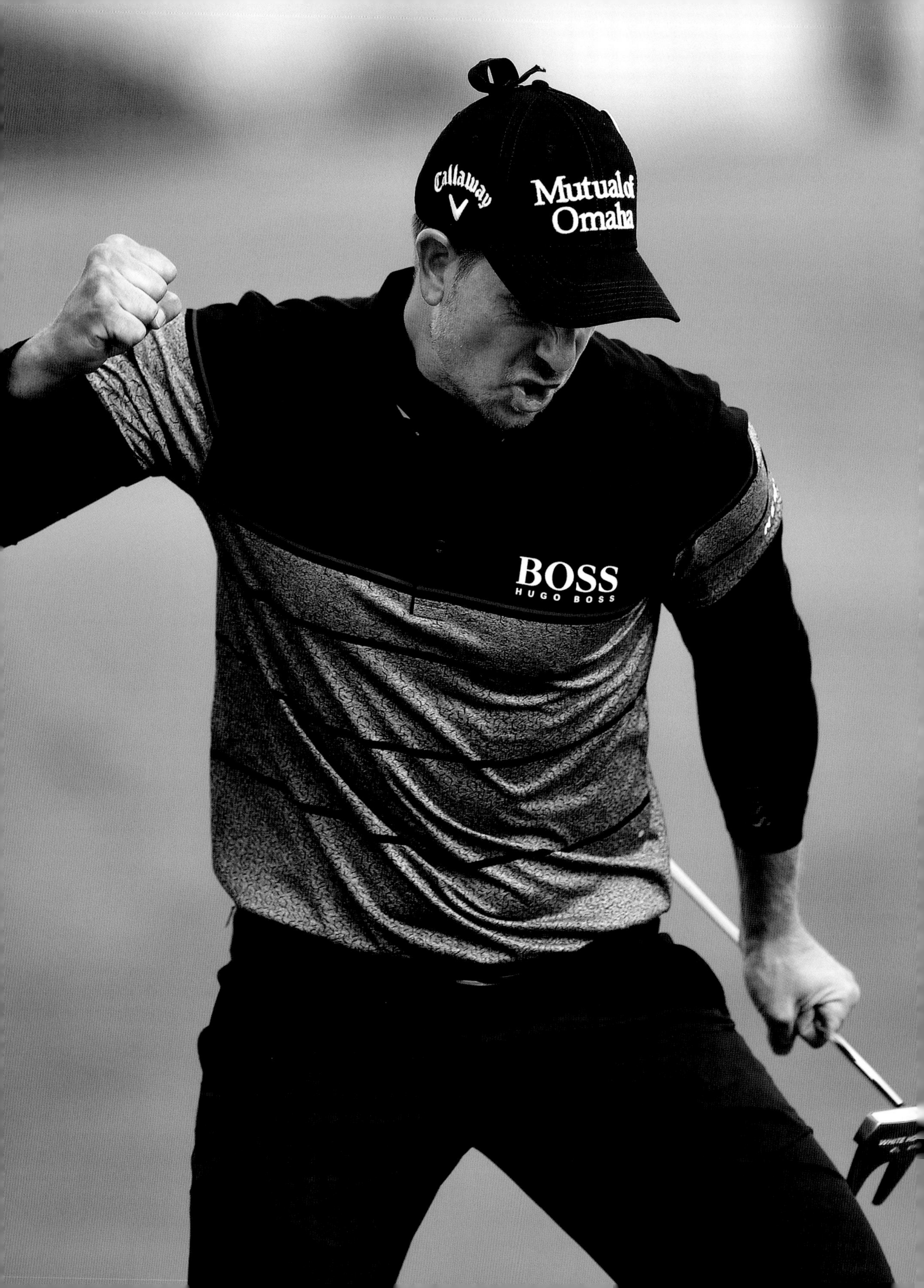
Callaway
Mutual of Omaha
BOSS
HUGO BOSS

Stenson Triumphs in Epic Duel

By Andy Farrell

In hindsight, announcing the result of Glenmorangie's search for the Greatest Open Finish on this Sunday was unfortunate timing. In the morning the news appeared no more than a statement of the obvious. By the end of the afternoon, it could be considered hopelessly premature.

From the previous 144 editions of The Open, the selection of the "Duel in the Sun," when Tom Watson pipped Jack Nicklaus after a 36-hole thriller at Turnberry in 1977, could be universally approved. Until The 145th Open had played out at Royal Troon and the contest between Henrik Stenson and Phil Mickelson became an equally worthy contender.

These two Ayrshire Opens, 39 years apart, stand out as Championships where two players battled head-to-head over the final two rounds, sepa-

rating themselves from the rest of the field with mesmerising play and record scoring, providing a see-saw contest with multiple changes of lead that captivated their on-lookers until the very end.

There may be minor differences. Meteorologically for a start, the clue in the title from 1977, The Open played in scorching sunshine, bar a brief thunderstorm, while this year it was blustery, overcast and occasionally wet, though the difficulty of the conditions only enhanced the quality attained by Stenson and Mickelson. Turnberry's participants might be considered more decorated, but no one can seriously denigrate the credentials of the first Swede to hold the Claret Jug and the five-time Major winner he defeated. And while Watson and Nicklaus produced pyrotechnics right to the very last hole, this latest tussle will always be remembered as being far tighter than the final winning margin of three strokes suggests.

A brief primer on 1977: Tied with Nicklaus after two rounds, although not leading until the third round, Watson went 65-65 over the last two rounds (played on Friday and Saturday back then), while his rival scored 65-66. Nicklaus led by three early in the final round but Watson holed from 60 feet

Henrik Stenson celebrates holing his long putt at the 15th.

EXCERPTS FROM THE PRESS

JB Holmes finished third to win the "other tournament."

at the 15th to draw level, went one ahead with one to play, and then hit his approach at the last to two feet. Nicklaus, whose second shot was from the base of a bush, was on the edge of the green but holed from 35 feet for a birdie that forced Watson to hole his tap-in to avoid a play-off. They left the 18th green arms about each other's shoulders, Watson having set a new record total of 268 in The Open, while Nicklaus finished 10 ahead of third-placed Hubert Green who said: "I won the tournament I played. They were playing in something else."

So to 2016 and here, too, were Stenson and Mickelson leaving the 18th green with their arms around each other's shoulders. It was only fitting after the pair had turned The 145th Open into their own exclusive weekend twosome, playing in the last pairing on both Saturday

Sergio Garcia, who went on to tie for fifth place, drives at the par-five sixth hole.

and Sunday. They had their own mutual appreciation for what the other had achieved. The rest of us were left dazzled and bewildered by what had just taken place in this "High Troon" showdown.

To win by three — the margin still feels too many — Stenson birdied four of the last five holes. He came home in 31 on Troon's fearsome back nine. He had 10 birdies in all. He scored a 63, as Mickelson had in the first round, to tie the Major record and beat Greg Norman's 64 from Royal St George's in 1993 as the lowest final round by a Champion Golfer of the Year. He set a new record to par for The Open of 20-under, beating Tiger Woods' 19-under-par from St Andrews in 2000. His winning total of 264 beat The Open record set by Norman in 1993 by three strokes and bettered by one the Major record set by David Toms at the 2001 PGA Championship.

In losing by three strokes — still too many — Mickelson scored a final round of 65, did not have bogey on his card and beat by two the previous lowest score by a runner-up of 269 by Nicklaus in

Rory McIlroy enjoyed his best round of the week with a 67 to finish tied for fifth.

1977, Nick Faldo at Royal St George's in 1993 and Jesper Parnevik at Turnberry in 1994. His total of 267 equalled the previous lowest for The Open, by Norman in 1993. He finished 11 strokes ahead of the man in third place, compatriot JB Holmes, who said: "Those guys were playing a different course to everyone else."

Was 2016 better than 1977? Is it even possible to say? The debate had only just got going when the definitive contribution was made by golf's highest authority, Nicklaus himself.

The Golden Bear posted on social media:

"I was fortunate to watch every second of today's final round of The Open Championship and I thought it was fantastic. Phil Mickelson played one of the best rounds I have ever seen played in The Open and Henrik Stenson just played better — he played one of the greatest rounds I have ever seen. Phil certainly has nothing to be ashamed of because he played wonderfully. Henrik played well from beginning to end. He drove the ball well; his iron game was great; his short game was wonderful; and his putting was great. Henrik was simply terrific. To win your first Major Championship is something special in and of itself, but to do it in the fashion Henrik did it in, makes for something very special and incredibly memorable. I'm proud of and happy for Henrik. Some in the media have already tried to compare today's final round to 1977 at Turnberry, with Tom Watson and me in what they called the "duel in the sun." I thought we played great and had a wonderful match. On that day, Tom got me, 65-66. Our final round was really good, but theirs was even better. What a great match today."

Tyrrell Hatton completes a 68 at the 18th to tie for fifth, the highest placed Englishman.

Hats off to Hatton after high finish

After missing the halfway cut in each of his four previous appearances in The Open, Tyrrell Hatton was determined to prove that he could perform on the biggest stage. And prove it, he did.

Hatton had rounds of 70, 71, 71 and 68 for a four-under-par total of 280 and a share of fifth place with Rory McIlroy and Sergio Garcia. It was the best performance by an Englishman at The Open since Ian Poulter and Lee Westwood tied for third behind Phil Mickelson at Muirfield in 2013 and was achieved with little fuss.

Apart from a double-bogey on the par-five fourth on the second day, 24-year-old Hatton dropped only four other shots all week at Royal Troon, which, remarkably, was fewer than the Champion Golfer of the Year Henrik Stenson.

"My best performances are on links courses," said Hatton, who finished runner-up at the Scottish Open at Castle Stuart the previous week. "I played a lot of links golf as an amateur. When conditions get tough, I can grind out a decent score, and thankfully my short game helped me out.

"The big thing today was the par putts I holed like at the eighth and ninth. That just kept the momentum going. The only blip was on 11, but that was the hardest hole on the course."

Hatton acknowledges that his emotions can get the better of him on the course. "I'm so passionate about wanting to do well and sometimes that just overspills," he said. Not this time, though. At Troon he was calmness personified.

Adam Scott, who finished 43rd, chips at the first hole on another blustery and rainy day.

Watson, the gracious five-time Champion Golfer of the Year that he is, concurred. Faldo, now Sir Nick, who saw his first Open while camping out at Troon in 1973, added: "We'll never see perfection on a links like that ever again in our times. This was another duel like Jack and Tom but they took it up a couple of notches."

Mickelson, who only accepted after six holes of the final round that it was simply between the two of them, said: "I don't remember being in a match like that where we've separated ourselves from the field by so many strokes. It was fun to be a part of that. It certainly crossed my mind a little bit out there today, that match when Jack and Tom went head-to-head in 1977. I know I wanted to be more Tom in that case than Jack, but unfortunately ... I understand how it feels. It's bittersweet, I guess."

Stenson said: "It was a great match with Phil. It seemed like it was going to be a two-horse race, and it was all the way to the end. I knew he wasn't going to back down at any point and in a way that made it easier for me. I knew I had to keep on pushing,

Dustin Johnson is relieved to finish.

Eagle for Mickelson at the fourth hole to tie Stenson.

Steve Stricker scored a 69 to finish fourth.

Thumbs up for new hero Andrew Johnston.

keep on giving myself birdie chances. He wasn't going to give it to me, so I had to pull away. I'm just delighted I managed to do that with a couple of birdies at the right time on the final stretch."

Mickelson added: "I was just trying to birdie every hole and it seemed like he was, too. I was just trying to keep pace. I had to make 30, 40-footers just to keep pace with him and wasn't able to do it at the end."

Stenson added: "We managed to pull away from the rest of the field and we both played some great golf. Phil has been one of the best to play the game, certainly in the last 20 years. So to come out on top after such a fight with him over these four days, it makes it even more special."

It was another blustery day on the Ayrshire coast and rainy, too, in the morning. But just as the leaders

Bill Haas still finished in the top 10 despite a closing 75.

EXCERPTS FROM THE PRESS

"'I was there,' will be the claim for years to come by those lucky enough to witness the great contest."

—Martin Dempster,
The Scotsman

"At the sixth, they had exactly the same yardage to the green, so they had to toss a coin to see who would hit first. The way they were playing it looked like that coin might be needed to decide who would go home with the Claret Jug."

—Paul Mahoney,
The Independent

"Henrik Stenson kept hitting the best shots of his life, one after another, because there was no other way to beat Phil Mickelson in an Open showdown that ranked among the best in golf."

—Bob Harig, ESPN.com

"You will often hear the pros talk about the different sound Stenson's iron shots make when they leave the blade and here he underlined exactly what they mean on the biggest stage of all."

—Derek Lawrenson,
Daily Mail

went off, the clouds parted and a weak sun made a reappearance. It seemed a higher authority than even Nicklaus wanted to watch this one.

While Stenson started the day at 12-under-par, and Mickelson at 11-under, no other player got past seven-under-par all day. Bill Haas had been the nearest challenger, but he never had a birdie in a 75. Andrew "Beef" Johnston had a terrific start, with three birdies and a bogey in the first four holes to get to seven-under-par.

But that was as good as it got for the Londoner, though he was still thoroughly enjoying himself, as you would scoring 73 to finish eighth in The Open, and the crowds were still warming to their folk hero. There were tears of joy as cancer-survivor Matthew Southgate finished in a tie for 12th. Twice a winner from Final Qualifying in the last three years, he will be excused from doing so in 2017 with an exemption straight to Royal Birkdale.

So, too, Tyrrell Hatton, who only made it to Troon by finishing second in the Scottish Open at Castle Stuart the week before. A

Even on the hardest holes, as here at 11, Mickelson and Stenson kept hitting quality shots.

closing 68 put the young Englishman into a tie for fifth with Sergio Garcia and Rory McIlroy, who returned his best round of the week with a 67.

In fact, each of the leading four players had played at Castle Stuart, including Holmes and Steve Stricker, the 49-year-old veteran, who still plays remarkable golf on a limited schedule. Both finished with 69s to be six and five-under-par respectively. It would have been a good battle for the "other tournament." Neither made a bogey, but each made a late double. Holmes took six at the 15th but claimed a stroke back at the next, while Stricker had a five at the 17th.

It was a reminder that just one false swing could lead to disaster. The proof was there on everyone else's scorecards but for the two in the final pairing. Under the intense pressure of playing for The Open, let alone that exerted on each other by their stellar play, there was hardly a false step from either of them. The only two bogeys came from Stenson and were the result of three-putting from long distance. It only adds to the madness that the 10th time a 63 was scored in The Open, it began with a three-putt.

After twice having a two-shot swing go in his favour late on Saturday, Stenson suffered the reverse when he failed to give either his approach or his first putt enough oomph at the first hole. "It is never great when you three-putt and your opponent sticks it to a foot," Stenson said.

Mickelson, who had shown his intention of claiming the Claret Jug for a second time by placing his hand on the trophy's protective cover as it sat on its plinth on the first tee, opened with a perfect eight-iron approach to retake the lead at the first opportunity. "That wasn't the start I was looking for," Stenson admitted, "but more important was what happened afterwards. I was sticking to my game plan and committing to my shots."

He birdied the next three holes, making a couple

A birdie for Stenson at the 14th to retake the lead.

Søren Kjeldsen saved par from the rough at the 16th and recorded his first top 10 at The Open.

Martin Kaymer escapes at the fourth.

of 15-footers at the second and third holes and two-putting for a four at the fourth. Mickelson had seen his chip from over the bunkers on the right of the second green hit the flagstick but not go in. But at the fourth he launched a four-iron to 12 feet and made the eagle. All tied again.

Both birdied the par-five sixth, but the short eighth, so good to the American on the first two days, favoured the Swede now as Stenson holed from 15 feet for a two. As you were at the turn, both out in 32, Stenson leading by one.

One thing might yet have to change. As a result of a standing bet, should Stenson win a Major, his caddie Gareth Lord would have to give up smoking. As Lord lit up on the seventh, Stenson told him: "Enjoy that. You have about two and a half hours left."

The most dangerous part of the course arrived with the thought that it would be sad if one miscue now had a disproportionate impact on the result. Clearly neither of the players were thinking anything of the sort. Both birdied the 10th from around 15 feet and the only damage at the 11th was when Stenson three-putted from 40 feet. Tied again, Mickelson barely saw the fairway at the 12th but, as with the previous day, made a sporty par-saver, this time from 18 feet.

So to the 14th, where Stenson had swung things in his favour

Patrick Reed found trouble on the fourth but finished tied for 12th.

Zach Johnson all wrapped up.

on Saturday. A six-iron to 20 feet, followed by a single putt, and he retook the lead. "It was a key moment again," he said. "I just thought, 'How many chances coming in am I going to have to pull away?' I knew I had to take it. And then made an absolute bomb on 15."

It was from over 50 feet across the 15th green, the blow that put the Swede two ahead as Mickelson had little chance of matching it. "I needed to knock mine in on top of him, just follow suit," Mickelson said. "But I had a 40-45 footer to try and do that."

There was still hope, however, at the par-five 16th. Mickelson put a three-wood onto the green, 40 feet away. Stenson had to chip with his third shot and put it to five feet. Mickelson couldn't bring off another piece of Lefty magic, could he?

His putt looked really good all the way. "I thought I could get one back and be only one down with two difficult holes to go. I don't know how that eagle putt missed. I really thought it was going in." His mind may have gone back to the 18th on Thursday. "There were a couple of putts like this week. I've made a bunch, too, but a couple of critical ones caught the lip."

From the possibility of gaining one, or even two shots, Mickelson's four did not gain him any ground as Stenson marched up and holed his birdie putt. "That was huge. You expect Phil to make every putt, you have to, and his eagle putt looked like it was going in. It just snuck by and I'm standing over a five-footer down the hill to keep two ahead. That was a very important putt to make."

Colin Montgomerie at the 18th of his home club: "I've been the leader in the clubhouse again, second time this week!"

Stenson's putt at the 15th put the Swede two ahead.

On the way to the 17th tee, Stenson tried to find a secluded spot to take off his undershirt. "I'm a little hot," he told nearby spectators, who speculated whether he meant his body or his golf. It was not quite Nicklaus taking off his sweater before driving the 18th green at St Andrews all those years ago, but Stenson knew the tee shot at the 17th was a crucial moment. Another peerless four-iron finished six feet away. Mickelson missed the green but saved par. Stenson could have sewn it up completely had he made the putt, but it missed.

There was to be one last chance for a birdie at the last, however. And this time his 30-footer was sucked into the hole. It was only the second time ever that a final-round 63 had won a Major, Johnny Miller at Oakmont in 1973 the only other player to do it. It also meant, on a course where it is usually advisable to make your score on the way out and cling to it on the way home, Stenson had played each of the halves in 10-under-par for the week. While the outward half played to its

Another putt Mickelson thought he had holed but his eagle effort at the 16th just missed.

par for the week, the second nine had averaged two-over-par per day — so, on average, Stenson had gained 18 strokes on the field coming home.

Afterwards, Stenson dedicated the victory to a friend, Mike Gerbich, who had died on the eve of the Championship. Stenson added: "I felt like this was going to be my turn. It's not something you want to run around and shout about. I knew I was going to have to battle, but I think it was that extra self-belief that made me go all the way this week."

Nine times he had been second or third in a Major, but now he had his first victory, and Sweden's first, too. Parnevik, a runner-up in The Open in 1994 and 1997, had sent him a message: "Go out and finish what I couldn't finish."

"I feel very privileged to be the one to hold this trophy," Stenson said, also admitting that

Stenson acknowledges the gallery walking up the 18th.

Round of the Day: **Phil Mickelson – 65**

OFFICIAL SCORECARD
THE 145TH OPEN
ROYAL TROON

Phil MICKELSON
Game 41
Sunday 17 July at 2:35pm

FOR R&A USE ONLY 41.1

54 HOLE TOTAL	202	ROUND 4
THIS ROUND	65	72 HOLE TOTAL
72 HOLE TOTAL	267	267

ROUND 4

Hole	1	2	3	4	5	6	7	8	9	Out	10	11	12	13	14	15	16	17	18	In	Total
Yards	367	390	377	555	209	601	401	123	422	3445	451	482	430	473	178	499	554	220	458	3745	7190
Par	4	4	4	5	3	5	4	3	4	36	4	4	4	4	3	4	5	3	4	35	71
Score	3	4	4	3	3	4	4	3	4	32	3	4	4	4	3	4	4	3	4	33	65

Signature of Marker

VERIFIED

Signature of Competitor

Phil Mickelson

being asked when Sweden's men would make the breakthrough had got annoying over the years. What might the 40-year-old go on to achieve? "We're only just getting started, aren't we? You never know once you open the floodgates what might happen."

But that was for the future. For now, it was a time to savour the moment after all the hard work and dedication, the downs as well as the ups, the fulfilment of his greatest golfing desire.

"It's a dream come true," he said. "I was 11 when I started playing. The Ryder Cup and The Open, those were the big early memories I had. So to sit here and hold this trophy is really amazing."

So, too, this epic duel. Whether it was the greatest finish in The Open, or just one of them, hardly mattered. It was a day when Mickelson excelled but Stenson triumphed.

A gracious runner-up once again

Phil Mickelson has won five Major Championships and has now finished runner-up 11 times. On the list on which he would rather not figure so highly, he moved past Arnold Palmer's 10 and lies behind only Jack Nicklaus' 19. After losing to Henrik Stenson in their titanic battle, he was as gracious as ever, if naturally a little bemused.

"Gosh, it is disappointing to come in second but I'm happy for Henrik. He's a really great Champion. We've been friends for some time. I've always thought that he is one of the best ball-strikers in the game and that Major Championships are perfectly suited to him. I knew that he would ultimately come through and win. I'm happy that he did. I'm disappointed that it was at my expense.

"It's probably the best I've played and not won. I think that's why it's disappointing. I can't say I should have done this or that. I played a bogey-free round of 65 in the final round of a Major, usually that's good enough, and I got beat. I got beat by 10 birdies. It's not like the other guys were doing the same thing. It was a challenging day.

"I'm excited by the work I've put in with my coach, Andrew Getson, that I was able to hit the fairways coming down the stretch. I'm proud of the way I played.

"I feel I played well enough to win this Championship by a number of strokes. It's not like I've got decades left of opportunities to win Majors, so each one means a lot to me."

Round of the Day: **Henrik Stenson – 63**

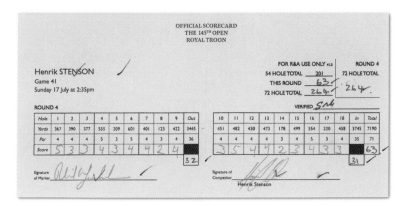

It's a
FACT

Henrik Stenson became only the fourth Champion Golfer of the Year to score all four rounds under 70 in The Open following Greg Norman at Royal St George's in 1993, Nick Price at Turnberry in 1994 and Tiger Woods at St Andrews in 2000. Four others have achieved the feat without winning.

CHAMPIONSHIP HOLE SUMMARY

HOLE	PAR	YARDS	EAGLES	BIRDIES	PARS	BOGEYS	D.BOGEYS	OTHER	RANK	AVERAGE
1	4	367	0	70	330	66	6	0	12	4.017
2	4	390	0	56	313	92	8	3	10	4.129
3	4	377	1	88	321	54	7	1	15	3.966
4	5	555	8	175	238	43	8	0	18	4.720
5	3	209	0	53	299	112	8	0	8	3.159
6	5	601	7	108	279	66	11	1	16	4.934
7	4	401	0	102	291	71	6	2	14	3.972
8	3	123	0	87	290	74	11	10	11	3.089
9	4	422	0	52	309	93	15	3	7	4.169
OUT	36	3,445	16	791	2,670	671	80	20		36.157
10	4	451	0	23	285	137	22	5	3	4.369
11	4	482	0	24	262	125	35	26	1	4.559
12	4	430	0	29	308	119	11	5	4	4.275
13	4	473	1	38	306	113	10	3	6	4.219
14	3	178	1	76	319	70	5	0	13	3.004
15	4	499	0	32	260	145	27	7	2	4.403
16	5	554	7	140	273	37	13	1	17	4.813
17	3	220	0	30	318	107	15	1	5	3.234
18	4	458	0	50	325	82	12	2	9	4.132
IN	35	3,745	9	442	2,656	935	150	50		37.008
TOTAL	71	7,190	25	1,233	5,326	1,606	230	70		73.161

FOURTH ROUND LEADERS

HOLE	1	2	3	4	5	6	7	8	9	10	11	12	13	14	15	16	17	18	TOTAL
PAR	4	4	4	5	3	5	4	3	4	4	4	4	4	3	4	5	3	4	TOTAL
Henrik Stenson	5	3	3	4	3	4	4	2	4	3	5	4	4	2	3	4	3	3	63-264
Phil Mickelson	3	4	4	3	3	4	4	3	4	3	4	4	4	3	4	4	3	4	65-267
JB Holmes	4	4	4	4	3	4	3	3	4	4	4	4	3	6	4	3	4	4	69-278
Steve Stricker	4	4	4	4	3	5	3	3	4	4	4	4	4	2	4	4	5	4	69-279
Rory McIlroy	4	3	4	5	2	4	4	3	3	4	5	5	3	3	4	4	3	4	67-280
Tyrrell Hatton	3	4	4	5	3	5	3	3	4	4	5	3	4	3	4	4	3	4	68-280
Sergio Garcia	4	4	4	4	3	5	3	2	4	5	4	4	5	3	4	4	3	4	69-280
Andrew Johnston	3	5	3	4	3	5	4	4	4	5	4	5	4	3	5	5	3	4	73-281

■ EAGLE OR BETTER ■ BIRDIES ■ BOGEYS ■ DBL BOGEYS/WORSE

SCORING SUMMARY

FOURTH ROUND SCORES

Players Under Par	21
Players At Par	9
Players Over Par	51

CHAMPIONSHIP SCORES

Rounds Under Par	104
Rounds At Par	53
Rounds Over Par	314

LOW SCORES

Low First Nine

Henrik Stenson	32
Phil Mickelson	32
Rory McIlroy	32
Lee Westwood	32

Low Second Nine

Henrik Stenson	31

Low Round

Henrik Stenson	63

FOURTH ROUND HOLE SUMMARY

HOLE	PAR	YARDS	EAGLES	BIRDIES	PARS	BOGEYS	D.BOGEYS	OTHER	RANK	AVERAGE
1	4	367	0	10	51	19	1	0	10	4.136
2	4	390	0	5	58	17	1	0	7	4.173
3	4	377	0	20	57	3	1	0	16	3.815
4	5	555	4	32	38	7	0	0	18	4.593
5	3	209	0	6	49	24	2	0	4	3.272
6	5	601	1	14	49	15	2	0	13	5.037
7	4	401	0	22	51	7	1	0	15	3.840
8	3	123	0	13	50	14	2	2	9	3.148
9	4	422	0	2	62	14	3	0	6	4.222
OUT	36	3,445	5	124	465	120	13	2		36.235
10	4	451	0	6	57	17	1	0	8	4.160
11	4	482	0	4	44	26	4	3	1	4.519
12	4	430	0	2	50	25	2	2	2	4.420
13	4	473	1	10	52	17	1	0	12	4.086
14	3	178	0	10	59	12	0	0	14	3.025
15	4	499	0	4	48	24	4	1	3	4.383
16	5	554	3	32	42	2	2	0	17	4.605
17	3	220	0	2	58	19	2	0	5	3.259
18	4	458	0	5	65	8	3	0	11	4.111
IN	35	3,745	4	75	475	150	19	6		36.568
TOTAL	71	7,190	9	199	940	270	32	8		72.802

" It's not something you want to run around and shout, but I felt like this was going to be my turn. "
—Henrik Stenson

" The Claret Jug's a pretty awesome thing. I'd love to get my hands on it again, but I'm sure Henrik will let me drink out of it again if I need to. "
—Zach Johnson

" If you would have told me heading into the week I'd have a legitimate chance to finish in the top five, I don't know if I would have believed you. "
—Steve Stricker

" You've always got to remember where you've come from and where you've been. I always stay grounded. I'll always be the same person. That's the most important thing. "
—Andrew Johnston

" I gained some momentum today. For the first time all week I saw some putts from six feet go in. "
—Jordan Spieth

" It's going to be a top-five finish, so there's not much wrong. I want to win, but I think you guys are more desperate for it to happen than I am. "
—Rory McIlroy

" We're all here to try to do one job and that's win — and unfortunately this is the only Major Championship where you have to battle the elements. "
—Jason Day

" I've been the leader in the clubhouse again, second time this week! "
—Colin Montgomerie

From despair to Open glory

John Hopkins salutes the character of Sweden's first Champion Golfer of the Year

There are many reasons to admire Henrik Stenson — for his golf, his mischievous sense of humour, his devotion to his family, the professionalism with which he goes about his work — but perhaps the greatest is that the consummate demonstration of skill he gave at Royal Troon came after he had recovered from falling deep into a golfing slough of depression.

Let us return to the summer of 2001, a time when Tiger Woods, by capturing that April's Masters, had completed the remarkable feat of winning the four professional Major Championships in a row. While Woods was in his pomp on one side of the Atlantic, Stenson was in despair on the other.

In the second week of May, Stenson, three years after he had turned professional, won the Benson and Hedges International at The Belfry. Yet by the

end of the first week in July he had lost his game to such an extent that he needed three attempts to keep his first drive in play at the European Open. Golf is full of those who have lost their form quickly, but to do it in 50 days is remarkable.

Enter the man who could be called the players' coach. Pete Cowen had been on tour for six or seven years, a familiar figure on the practice grounds. Dressed from head to toe in black, he would work quietly with players such as Darren Clarke or Lee Westwood, charging them no fees but a small percentage of their winnings if they finished in the top 10.

It is just as well for Cowen that Clarke and Westwood were winning tournaments, because he wasn't making any money from Stenson. "He couldn't play at all when we first started working together," Cowen said. "He couldn't hit a golf course, never mind find a fairway. I told him it might take one year, 18 months, 24 months. He said: 'Okay. Let's do it.'"

Cowen soon noticed that Stenson was exceptionally disciplined. "He would do what I asked him to do with greater determination than anyone I have ever met," Cowen said. "If I said to him, 'You have to practise that shot all day and nothing else,' he would. He would have practised it all night too if I had asked him to."

Ingemar Stenson, Henrik's father, was a worried man at this time. "He was 25 and had been playing golf for nearly 15 years, yet he was prepared to put himself through all that again in order to improve."

Soon, though, his concern turned to pride. "Henrik is stubborn," Ingemar said. "When he was 12 he told his soccer coach he wanted to give up soccer. The coach asked to speak to me to see if I had any influence with Henrik. I said: 'You heard him. He never changes his mind.' He didn't then and he does not now."

Such single-minded determination to follow

Cowen's teaching principles brought him an ability to hit crisp iron shots that were reminiscent of Tiger's — a rifle-like crack followed by a distinctive whistle as the ball pierced the air at nearly 200mph. With that came success, slowly at first, one victory on the European Tour in 2004, two in 2006 and 2007, and then the big prize of the Players Championship in the US in 2009.

Two other events in 2009 guaranteed him some attention: He stripped down to his underpants to play a shot in the WGC event at Doral (he and Fanny Sunesson, his caddie, wondered what all the fuss was about); and about the same time he lost millions of dollars in a Ponzi scheme operated by Allen Stanford. There were Ryder Cup appearances in 2006, 2008 and 2014, success in the 2013 Tour Championship and the FedExCup in the US, and the Race to Dubai in Europe. Now the man who couldn't hit a fairway in 2001, couldn't miss one.

Throughout it all Cowen was by his side. A bluff, no-nonsense Yorkshireman, Cowen became inordinately fond of Stenson. "My wife says he's like a third son to me," Cowen said on the practice ground at Royal Troon, having just wished Stenson good luck for the last round of The Open.

As Stenson battled with Mickelson to produce the greatest finishing round in a Major, Cowen was driving south to his home in Sheffield. "My stomach was in knots all the way," he said. "I won't do that again. But it was special wasn't it?"

So by all means salute Stenson for playing the most stupendous closing round of golf ever, but salute him as much for the strength of character he showed to come back from hitting tee shots an amateur would have been embarrassed by.

Golf is said to be a game played both on the ground and between the ears, and rarely has this been shown to be more true than on a Sunday afternoon at Royal Troon in July 2016.

The 145th Open

Complete Scores

HOLE			1	2	3	4	5	6	7	8	9	10	11	12	13	14	15	16	17	18			
PAR	POS		4	4	4	4	5	4	4	3	4	4	3	4	4	5	4	4	4	4		TOTAL	
Henrik Stenson	T12	Rd 1	4	4	4	5	3	3	4	3	4	4	5	3	5	2	4	4	3	4	68		
Sweden	2	Rd 2	4	4	3	4	2	5	3	3	5	3	4	4	3	3	4	4	3	4	65		
£1,175,000	1	Rd 3	3	4	3	4	3	6	4	4	4	4	4	4	2	4	5	2	4		68		
	1	Rd 4	5	3	3	4	3	4	4	2	4	3	5	4	4	2	3	4	3	3	63	-20	**264**
Phil Mickelson	1	Rd 1	4	3	4	4	3	4	4	2	4	3	4	4	4	2	4	4	2	4	63		
USA	1	Rd 2	4	4	4	4	3	5	3	2	4	4	4	5	4	2	5	5	3	4	69		
£675,000	2	Rd 3	4	4	3	5	3	5	4	3	4	4	4	4	3	4	4	4	4	4	70		
	2	Rd 4	3	4	4	3	3	4	4	3	4	3	4	4	4	3	4	4	3	4	65	-17	**267**
JB Holmes	T35	Rd 1	3	4	4	4	3	4	4	3	4	4	5	4	6	2	5	4	3	4	70		
USA	T15	Rd 2	3	4	4	5	3	5	3	4	4	4	4	4	2	6	4	3	4		70		
£433,000	5	Rd 3	3	3	4	5	2	5	4	3	3	4	4	4	4	5	5	3	4		69		
	3	Rd 4	4	4	4	4	3	4	3	3	4	4	4	4	3	6	4	3	4		69	-6	**278**
Steve Stricker	T4	Rd 1	4	5	4	4	2	5	4	3	3	5	4	4	2	4	4	3	3		67		
USA	T27	Rd 2	4	4	4	5	3	5	4	3	4	4	4	4	3	8	5	3	4		75		
£337,000	T6	Rd 3	4	5	3	4	4	4	4	3	3	4	4	4	3	4	4	3	4		68		
	4	Rd 4	4	4	4	4	3	5	3	3	4	4	4	4	2	4	4	5	4		69	-5	**279**
Rory McIlroy	T22	Rd 1	4	4	4	4	3	4	3	2	4	4	4	4	6	4	3	5	3	4	69		
Northern Ireland	T15	Rd 2	4	3	4	5	3	4	3	3	5	5	4	5	5	3	4	4	3	4	71		
£235,667	T18	Rd 3	5	4	5	4	4	4	4	3	4	4	4	4	3	5	5	5	3	4	73		
	T5	Rd 4	4	3	4	5	2	4	4	3	3	4	5	5	3	3	4	4	3	4	67	-4	**280**
Tyrrell Hatton	T35	Rd 1	4	4	4	5	3	5	4	2	3	4	4	4	4	4	4	5	3	4	70		
England	T22	Rd 2	4	4	4	7	3	4	4	2	4	4	4	4	4	3	3	5	4	4	71		
£235,667	T13	Rd 3	4	4	4	5	3	5	4	2	4	4	4	4	5	3	4	5	3	4	71		
	T5	Rd 4	3	4	4	5	3	5	3	3	4	5	3	4	3	4	4	4	3	4	68	-4	**280**
Sergio Garcia	T12	Rd 1	4	3	4	4	3	5	5	3	3	4	5	3	4	2	4	4	4	4	68		
Spain	T6	Rd 2	4	4	4	5	3	4	4	3	4	4	4	5	4	2	4	4	3	5	70		
£235,667	T9	Rd 3	4	4	3	6	3	5	3	2	4	5	4	5	5	2	6	5	3	4	73		
	T5	Rd 4	4	4	4	4	3	5	3	2	4	5	4	4	5	3	4	4	3	4	69	-4	**280**
Andrew Johnston	T22	Rd 1	4	4	4	7	3	4	4	3	4	3	3	4	4	4	3	5	3	3	69		
England	T6	Rd 2	5	5	3	4	2	5	4	2	4	4	7	4	4	3	3	4	2	4	69		
£170,000	4	Rd 3	4	4	4	5	3	5	3	3	3	5	4	4	3	4	4	5	3	4	70		
	8	Rd 4	3	5	3	4	3	5	4	4	4	5	4	5	4	3	5	5	3	4	73	-3	**281**
Dustin Johnson	T51	Rd 1	5	4	4	5	3	4	3	3	4	4	4	4	3	4	6	3	4		71		
USA	T15	Rd 2	4	3	4	4	3	5	6	2	4	4	6	4	3	3	4	2	4		69		
£135,333	T13	Rd 3	4	4	4	4	3	5	3	3	3	4	7	4	5	3	4	5	3	4	72		
	T9	Rd 4	4	4	3	6	3	5	4	3	4	4	4	4	3	3	4	5	3	4	70	-2	**282**

*Denotes amateur

HOLE			1	2	3	4	5	6	7	8	9	10	11	12	13	14	15	16	17	18			TOTAL
PAR	POS		4	4	4	4	5	4	4	3	4	4	3	4	4	5	4	4	4	4			
Søren Kjeldsen	T4	Rd 1	4	3	4	4	4	4	4	2	4	4	4	5	4	3	4	4	3	3	67		
Denmark	T3	Rd 2	4	4	4	4	3	4	4	3	4	4	4	4	4	3	4	5	2	4	68		
£135,333	T6	Rd 3	4	4	5	4	4	4	3	4	4	6	5	4	5	4	4	4	3	4	75		
	T9	Rd 4	4	5	4	5	4	5	4	2	4	4	4	4	4	3	4	5	3	4	72	-2	**282**
Bill Haas	T12	Rd 1	4	3	4	4	4	6	3	3	4	4	4	5	4	2	4	4	3	4	68		
USA	T6	Rd 2	3	4	4	5	4	5	3	3	4	4	4	5	4	3	5	4	2	4	70		
£135,333	3	Rd 3	3	4	4	4	4	4	4	2	5	4	4	4	4	3	5	4	3	4	69		
	T9	Rd 4	4	4	4	5	4	6	4	4	4	4	5	4	4	3	4	5	3	4	75	-2	**282**
Matthew Southgate	T51	Rd 1	4	3	4	4	3	5	3	4	4	4	5	5	5	3	4	5	3	3	71		
England	T27	Rd 2	4	3	4	5	3	5	5	3	5	4	4	4	4	3	4	5	3	3	71		
£92,625	T25	Rd 3	4	4	4	4	3	5	5	3	4	5	4	4	5	2	5	4	3	4	72		
	T12	Rd 4	4	4	4	3	4	5	4	3	5	4	4	3	3	3	4	4	4	4	69	-1	**283**
Andy Sullivan	T4	Rd 1	4	3	4	4	4	6	3	2	4	4	4	3	4	3	5	4	3	3	67		
England	T41	Rd 2	4	5	4	5	2	5	7	4	4	4	4	4	5	4	4	4	3	4	76		
£92,625	T25	Rd 3	4	4	4	4	3	4	5	3	4	5	3	4	4	4	4	5	3	4	71		
	T12	Rd 4	3	4	3	4	3	6	4	4	4	4	3	4	4	3	4	5	3	4	69	-1	**283**
Emiliano Grillo	T22	Rd 1	4	4	4	5	3	5	4	3	4	4	4	5	4	3	3	4	2	4	69		
Argentina	T22	Rd 2	4	4	4	5	3	5	4	3	4	5	5	4	4	3	3	5	3	4	72		
£92,625	T18	Rd 3	4	5	4	4	4	4	4	4	4	4	4	5	4	2	4	5	3	4	72		
	T12	Rd 4	4	4	3	5	3	5	4	3	4	4	4	4	5	3	4	4	3	4	70	-1	**283**
Gary Woodland	T22	Rd 1	4	4	5	4	2	5	4	3	4	4	4	4	4	3	4	5	3	3	69		
USA	T27	Rd 2	4	4	4	5	4	5	4	2	5	5	4	4	4	3	4	5	3	4	73		
£92,625	T18	Rd 3	4	4	3	5	3	5	4	3	4	3	6	4	4	4	5	4	2	4	71		
	T12	Rd 4	3	4	4	4	3	6	4	4	5	3	4	4	3	3	4	5	3	4	70	-1	**283**
Zach Johnson	T4	Rd 1	3	3	4	4	3	5	4	2	4	4	4	4	4	2	4	4	4	5	67		
USA	5	Rd 2	4	3	4	4	4	4	4	2	4	4	5	4	3	3	5	5	3	5	70		
£92,625	T13	Rd 3	4	3	4	5	5	5	4	3	4	6	4	4	4	3	4	5	3	5	75		
	T12	Rd 4	4	4	3	4	3	5	4	3	4	4	4	4	4	3	6	5	3	4	71	-1	**283**
Patrick Reed	T2	Rd 1	4	4	2	4	3	4	3	3	4	5	4	3	5	3	4	5	3	3	66		
USA	T15	Rd 2	4	4	4	5	2	5	4	4	4	5	5	4	4	3	5	6	2	4	74		
£92,625	T9	Rd 3	4	5	4	4	2	4	3	4	4	5	4	3	4	3	5	5	3	5	71		
	T12	Rd 4	4	5	4	6	3	5	3	3	4	4	4	5	4	3	4	5	2	4	72	-1	**283**
Miguel A Jiménez	T51	Rd 1	5	5	4	5	3	5	4	3	6	4	4	4	3	4	3	4	2	4	71		
Spain	T41	Rd 2	4	4	3	5	4	4	4	3	4	4	5	6	4	3	3	5	3	4	72		
£69,375	T18	Rd 3	4	4	4	5	2	5	4	3	4	4	4	5	4	3	4	5	2	4	70		
	T18	Rd 4	4	4	4	5	2	5	4	3	4	5	4	4	4	3	5	4	4	3	71	E	**284**
Keegan Bradley	T4	Rd 1	4	3	4	4	3	4	4	3	4	4	4	4	5	3	3	4	3	4	67		
USA	T3	Rd 2	4	4	3	4	3	5	3	3	4	4	5	5	4	2	3	5	3	4	68		
£69,375	T9	Rd 3	5	4	4	6	3	4	4	3	4	5	4	4	4	5	5	5	3	5	76		
	T18	Rd 4	5	4	4	5	4	6	4	3	4	4	4	4	4	3	4	4	3	4	73	E	**284**
Charl Schwartzel	T75	Rd 1	4	4	4	4	3	5	4	3	4	5	6	4	5	2	4	5	2	4	72		
South Africa	T6	Rd 2	3	4	3	4	2	5	3	3	4	5	4	5	3	2	4	5	3	4	66		
£69,375	T9	Rd 3	4	6	4	4	3	4	4	2	4	5	5	4	4	3	6	4	3	4	73		
	T18	Rd 4	3	4	4	4	4	6	4	4	5	4	4	4	4	3	4	4	4	4	73	E	**284**
Tony Finau	T4	Rd 1	4	4	4	4	2	5	4	3	4	4	4	4	3	3	4	5	3	3	67		
USA	T6	Rd 2	4	4	5	4	3	5	5	3	5	4	3	4	4	3	4	5	2	4	71		
£69,375	T6	Rd 3	4	4	4	4	3	4	6	4	4	4	5	4	4	2	4	5	3	4	72		
	T18	Rd 4	3	4	5	5	3	6	3	3	5	4	5	5	4	3	4	4	5	3	74	E	**284**

HOLE			1	2	3	4	5	6	7	8	9	10	11	12	13	14	15	16	17	18		TOTAL
PAR	POS		4	4	4	4	5	4	4	3	4	4	3	4	4	5	4	4	4	4		TOTAL
Lee Westwood	T51	Rd 1	4	4	5	5	3	5	3	4	5	5	4	3	4	3	4	3	3	4	71	
England	T50	Rd 2	4	4	4	4	3	6	4	3	5	3	4	4	4	4	4	5	4	4	73	
£52,406	T43	Rd 3	5	4	4	4	3	4	4	2	4	4	5	4	5	3	5	6	3	4	73	
	T22	Rd 4	3	4	3	5	3	4	3	3	4	5	4	4	5	3	4	4	3	4	68	+1 **285**
Jason Dufner	T51	Rd 1	4	3	4	5	4	5	3	3	3	4	4	4	4	3	4	5	4	5	71	
USA	T27	Rd 2	4	4	4	6	3	5	4	3	4	4	5	3	3	3	4	5	3	4	71	
£52,406	T39	Rd 3	5	4	4	6	3	5	4	3	5	4	4	3	3	3	5	4	5		74	
	T22	Rd 4	5	4	3	5	2	4	4	2	4	4	4	5	4	3	4	4	4	4	69	+1 **285**
David Howell	T110	Rd 1	4	5	4	6	3	5	4	3	4	4	3	4	3	5	5	5	3	5	74	
England	T50	Rd 2	4	5	4	5	4	5	4	2	3	4	4	4	3	4	4	3	4		70	
£52,406	T34	Rd 3	4	4	4	4	3	5	4	3	4	4	4	4	2	5	5	5	3	5	71	
	T22	Rd 4	4	4	4	5	3	4	3	3	4	4	5	4	4	3	4	5	3	4	70	+1 **285**
Justin Rose	T12	Rd 1	4	4	4	4	3	5	5	3	3	4	4	4	4	3	3	4	3	4	68	
England	T58	Rd 2	5	4	4	7	3	5	4	3	5	4	4	4	3	4	5	3	6		77	
£52,406	T34	Rd 3	4	4	4	5	2	4	3	4	4	4	4	3	3	4	7	3	4		70	
	T22	Rd 4	3	4	4	5	4	5	4	2	4	4	4	4	3	5	4	3	4		70	+1 **285**
Jason Day	T94	Rd 1	4	4	3	5	4	4	4	4	5	4	4	4	3	4	5	3	5		73	
Australia	T41	Rd 2	5	4	3	5	2	4	3	3	4	4	5	4	3	4	6	3	4		70	
£52,406	T25	Rd 3	4	3	4	4	3	5	3	3	3	5	4	5	3	5	5	3	5		71	
	T22	Rd 4	4	4	3	5	3	5	4	3	5	4	5	5	4	2	4	4	3	4	71	+1 **285**
Thongchai Jaidee	T51	Rd 1	4	4	4	5	3	4	4	3	4	4	4	4	4	3	6	5	3	3	71	
Thailand	T58	Rd 2	4	5	3	5	3	5	4	3	4	4	6	5	4	3	4	5	2	5	74	
£52,406	T25	Rd 3	4	3	4	5	2	5	4	4	3	4	4	4	5	3	5	4	3	3	69	
	T22	Rd 4	4	4	4	4	3	4	4	3	5	3	4	5	4	3	4	5	4	4	71	+1 **285**
Brandt Snedeker	T94	Rd 1	4	3	4	5	3	6	3	4	3	5	5	4	4	4	4	5	3	4	73	
USA	T67	Rd 2	4	4	4	5	3	6	3	3	5	4	4	5	4	3	4	5	4	3	73	
£52,406	T25	Rd 3	3	4	3	4	3	4	5	3	5	5	3	3	4	3	4	5	3	4	68	
	T22	Rd 4	4	4	3	6	4	5	5	3	4	4	3	4	3	4	4	4	3	4	71	+1 **285**
Kevin Na	T35	Rd 1	4	3	3	4	3	4	4	4	5	4	6	4	3	4	4	4	3	4	70	
USA	T11	Rd 2	5	4	4	6	2	4	3	3	5	4	4	3	4	3	4	5	3	3	69	
£52,406	T13	Rd 3	4	3	4	5	3	5	4	3	4	5	4	4	5	3	5	5	3	4	73	
	T22	Rd 4	4	4	4	4	4	5	4	3	4	5	5	5	3	3	4	4	3	5	73	+1 **285**
Jordan Spieth	T51	Rd 1	4	4	4	4	3	4	4	3	5	4	5	4	4	3	4	5	2	5	71	
USA	T67	Rd 2	5	4	4	4	3	6	4	5	4	4	4	5	4	2	5	5	3	4	75	
£39,042	T50	Rd 3	3	4	3	5	3	4	3	3	5	5	6	4	3	5	5	3	3	4	72	
	T30	Rd 4	4	4	4	3	3	5	4	4	3	3	4	4	3	5	4	3	4		68	+2 **286**
Russell Knox	T75	Rd 1	4	6	5	5	2	5	3	3	4	4	4	4	3	4	4	3	5	4	72	
Scotland	T27	Rd 2	4	5	4	4	2	5	4	3	4	3	4	4	4	3	4	5	4	4	70	
£39,042	T43	Rd 3	4	5	4	5	4	5	4	2	4	5	6	4	5	3	4	4	3	4	75	
	T30	Rd 4	4	4	4	4	4	5	3	3	4	4	4	4	3	4	4	4	3	4	69	+2 **286**
Darren Clarke	T51	Rd 1	4	5	3	6	3	4	4	3	3	4	4	5	3	4	4	3	4		71	
Northern Ireland	T41	Rd 2	4	4	4	5	2	5	3	4	5	4	4	5	5	3	4	5	3	3	72	
£39,042	T39	Rd 3	4	3	4	5	3	5	4	3	4	5	4	4	3	5	5	4	5		73	
	T30	Rd 4	4	5	4	4	4	5	4	2	4	4	5	4	2	3	4	3	5		70	+2 **286**
Ryan Palmer	T75	Rd 1	3	4	4	5	3	4	5	3	4	4	4	4	4	5	5	4	4	3	72	
USA	T58	Rd 2	4	4	4	6	3	5	4	2	4	5	4	5	5	3	4	4	4	3	73	
£39,042	T39	Rd 3	3	4	3	6	3	4	4	3	4	5	4	4	4	3	5	5	3	4	71	
	T30	Rd 4	4	4	4	4	3	3	4	3	5	4	4	5	4	3	4	5	3	4	70	+2 **286**

			1	2	3	4	5	6	7	8	9	10	11	12	13	14	15	16	17	18	
HOLE			1	2	3	4	5	6	7	8	9	10	11	12	13	14	15	16	17	18	
PAR	POS		4	4	4	4	5	4	4	3	4	4	3	4	4	5	4	4	4	4	TOTAL
Thomas Pieters	T12	Rd 1	3	4	3	5	3	5	4	4	4	4	4	4	4	2	4	4	3	4	68
Belgium	T50	Rd 2	4	3	4	5	4	8	3	3	5	4	6	4	4	3	4	4	4	4	76
£39,042	T25	Rd 3	4	4	4	4	3	5	3	3	5	4	4	4	4	3	4	4	4	4	70
	T30	Rd 4	4	4	3	4	3	5	4	2	4	5	9	4	4	3	4	3	3	4	72 +2 **286**
Haydn Porteous	T35	Rd 1	4	4	4	3	3	3	3	2	4	5	5	4	5	3	5	4	4	5	70
South Africa	T67	Rd 2	3	5	5	5	3	6	3	3	5	4	5	4	4	3	3	5	4	6	76
£39,042	T25	Rd 3	4	3	3	4	3	5	4	4	3	3	5	4	4	3	4	4	2	6	68
	T30	Rd 4	4	5	5	4	3	5	3	4	4	4	4	4	4	3	3	5	4	4	72 +2 **286**
Padraig Harrington	T35	Rd 1	4	4	4	4	3	4	4	5	4	5	4	4	3	4	4	4	2	4	70
Republic of Ireland	T27	Rd 2	5	4	4	4	3	5	5	3	4	3	5	4	4	3	4	4	3	5	72
£32,500	T34	Rd 3	4	4	4	5	3	4	5	3	5	5	4	4	5	3	4	5	3	3	73
	T36	Rd 4	4	4	4	6	3	7	4	2	4	4	4	4	4	3	4	4	3	4	72 +3 **287**
Martin Kaymer	T2	Rd 1	4	4	4	5	3	4	3	2	4	3	4	4	4	3	4	4	3	4	66
Germany	T11	Rd 2	4	5	4	4	3	5	4	2	3	7	5	4	4	3	4	5	3	4	73
£32,500	T18	Rd 3	4	5	5	5	3	4	3	3	3	5	4	6	4	3	5	5	4	3	74
	T36	Rd 4	4	4	4	5	2	5	5	3	5	4	4	4	4	4	4	5	4	4	74 +3 **287**
Francesco Molinari	T22	Rd 1	4	6	4	4	2	5	5	3	3	4	4	3	4	3	4	4	3	4	69
Italy	T15	Rd 2	4	3	4	5	3	4	4	3	5	4	4	5	4	3	3	5	4	4	71
£32,500	T18	Rd 3	4	5	3	5	4	5	4	3	4	5	4	4	4	3	4	5	3	4	73
	T36	Rd 4	4	4	4	4	3	5	4	3	4	4	4	6	4	3	5	5	4	4	74 +3 **287**
Bubba Watson	T35	Rd 1	3	4	3	4	2	4	4	6	4	5	5	4	4	2	4	5	4	3	70
USA	T67	Rd 2	5	4	5	4	4	5	4	3	4	5	6	4	5	2	4	5	4	3	76
£28,125	T50	Rd 3	5	4	3	4	3	5	3	3	5	5	7	3	4	3	4	4	3	4	72
	T39	Rd 4	5	4	4	5	4	3	3	3	4	4	4	4	4	4	4	3	3	4	70 +4 **288**
Matt Jones	T22	Rd 1	4	3	3	4	3	4	4	3	3	4	6	6	4	3	4	5	3	3	69
Australia	T27	Rd 2	6	4	4	5	3	5	3	3	4	5	4	5	4	2	4	5	3	4	73
£28,125	T43	Rd 3	4	4	4	5	4	5	5	2	4	4	5	5	3	5	5	4	3	4	75
	T39	Rd 4	4	4	4	4	3	5	4	3	4	5	5	5	2	4	4	4	3	4	71 +4 **288**
Rafa Cabrera Bello	T12	Rd 1	3	4	4	4	3	5	3	3	4	5	5	4	4	2	4	4	3	4	68
Spain	T11	Rd 2	3	4	5	5	4	5	4	2	4	4	3	4	4	3	5	5	3	4	71
£28,125	T25	Rd 3	4	4	3	5	3	5	3	4	4	5	5	4	3	6	5	5	3	5	75
	T39	Rd 4	5	4	4	5	4	6	3	3	4	5	5	4	4	4	4	3	3	4	74 +4 **288**
Webb Simpson	T35	Rd 1	4	4	3	5	3	6	3	2	3	5	4	4	5	3	4	5	3	4	70
USA	T27	Rd 2	5	4	5	5	3	6	5	2	4	4	4	4	3	4	4	4	2	4	72
£28,125	T18	Rd 3	4	4	4	4	3	5	4	3	4	5	5	3	4	3	5	4	4	3	71
	T39	Rd 4	5	4	4	5	4	5	3	3	4	4	6	4	3	3	5	5	3	5	75 +4 **288**
Adam Scott	T22	Rd 1	4	4	4	5	3	5	4	3	3	4	4	4	4	3	5	4	2	4	69
Australia	T27	Rd 2	4	4	4	5	3	5	4	3	4	5	5	4	5	3	3	5	3	4	73
£23,750	T50	Rd 3	6	4	4	5	3	5	3	3	3	4	6	4	4	3	4	5	4	6	76
	T43	Rd 4	4	4	3	5	3	4	5	3	3	5	4	5	4	3	5	4	3	4	71 +5 **289**
Luke Donald	T94	Rd 1	3	4	4	5	4	4	4	2	4	4	5	4	5	3	5	5	4	4	73
England	T58	Rd 2	3	5	6	5	2	5	5	2	5	4	4	4	4	3	5	4	3	3	72
£23,750	T43	Rd 3	4	4	4	4	4	5	4	4	4	4	4	4	5	3	4	5	2	4	72
	T43	Rd 4	4	5	4	5	3	6	4	2	4	4	4	4	5	3	4	4	2	5	72 +5 **289**
Jim Herman	T35	Rd 1	3	4	5	5	3	4	4	3	4	4	5	4	4	2	4	5	3	4	70
USA	T15	Rd 2	4	4	3	5	3	5	4	3	4	4	5	4	3	3	5	4	3	4	70
£23,750	T13	Rd 3	3	4	5	5	4	5	5	3	3	4	4	4	3	4	5	5	3	4	72
	T43	Rd 4	4	4	4	5	3	6	3	3	4	4	4	6	6	3	5	4	4	5	77 +5 **289**

HOLE			1	2	3	4	5	6	7	8	9	10	11	12	13	14	15	16	17	18		
PAR	POS		4	4	4	4	5	4	4	3	4	4	3	4	4	5	4	4	4	4		TOTAL
Harris English	T94	Rd 1	4	3	4	6	2	5	4	3	4	3	4	5	5	3	5	4	4	5	73	
USA	T67	Rd 2	4	4	4	5	4	5	4	3	3	4	4	5	5	4	5	4	3	3	73	
£19,129	T62	Rd 3	4	4	3	4	4	5	4	3	6	4	4	4	4	3	4	5	3	5	73	
	T46	Rd 4	4	4	4	5	4	4	4	2	4	5	4	5	3	3	4	5	3	4	71	+6 **290**
Richard Sterne	T12	Rd 1	4	4	4	4	4	4	3	3	3	4	3	4	5	3	4	5	3	4	68	
South Africa	T27	Rd 2	4	4	4	5	3	6	4	2	5	5	5	4	4	2	4	5	4	4	74	
£19,129	T50	Rd 3	4	4	3	5	4	6	5	3	3	5	5	4	4	4	5	5	3	4	76	
	T46	Rd 4	4	5	4	4	3	5	4	4	4	4	5	4	4	2	5	5	3	3	72	+6 **290**
Rickie Fowler	T22	Rd 1	4	4	3	4	3	5	4	3	4	4	4	5	4	2	4	5	3	4	69	
USA	T22	Rd 2	3	4	4	5	3	5	3	3	4	5	4	5	4	3	5	5	3	4	72	
£19,129	T43	Rd 3	4	3	4	4	3	6	5	3	4	4	8	4	4	4	5	4	3	4	76	
	T46	Rd 4	4	4	3	5	2	5	4	3	5	6	4	4	5	3	4	5	3	4	73	+6 **290**
Ryan Moore	T35	Rd 1	3	4	4	4	3	5	4	3	4	5	4	4	4	2	5	5	3	4	70	
USA	T41	Rd 2	4	4	4	4	4	5	5	3	4	3	4	5	4	3	4	5	3	5	73	
£19,129	T43	Rd 3	4	4	6	4	2	5	4	3	5	5	5	5	3	3	5	4	2	5	74	
	T46	Rd 4	5	4	4	4	3	5	4	3	4	4	4	4	4	3	5	5	4	4	73	+6 **290**
Alex Noren	T35	Rd 1	4	4	4	4	2	5	4	4	3	4	5	5	4	2	4	5	4	3	70	
Sweden	T27	Rd 2	4	4	4	5	3	5	4	3	5	4	4	4	4	2	5	5	3	4	72	
£19,129	T34	Rd 3	4	4	4	5	3	5	3	4	4	5	4	4	5	3	5	4	3	4	73	
	T46	Rd 4	5	4	3	6	3	6	4	3	5	4	4	4	5	2	4	5	4	4	75	+6 **290**
Nicolas Colsaerts	T75	Rd 1	4	3	4	4	3	4	4	4	3	5	4	4	5	3	5	4	5	4	72	
Belgium	T58	Rd 2	5	4	4	4	3	5	4	3	4	6	6	4	4	2	4	5	3	3	73	
£19,129	T34	Rd 3	4	4	4	4	3	5	3	2	4	4	4	4	5	3	5	5	3	4	70	
	T46	Rd 4	5	4	4	5	3	5	3	3	4	4	5	5	5	3	4	5	4	4	75	+6 **290**
Matt Kuchar	T51	Rd 1	4	4	3	5	4	5	4	2	5	4	3	3	4	3	4	5	4	5	71	
USA	T11	Rd 2	4	3	3	4	3	5	4	3	4	4	5	4	4	3	3	5	3	4	68	
£19,129	T25	Rd 3	4	5	4	5	3	7	4	3	3	4	4	4	5	3	5	4	3	5	75	
	T46	Rd 4	5	4	3	4	3	5	5	7	4	5	4	5	4	2	4	5	3	4	76	+6 **290**
Danny Willett	T51	Rd 1	4	4	3	4	3	4	4	3	4	5	5	5	4	3	4	5	3	4	71	
England	T67	Rd 2	5	4	4	6	3	5	3	5	4	5	4	4	4	4	4	4	3	4	75	
£16,760	T65	Rd 3	4	4	5	4	4	5	4	4	5	5	3	4	4	3	5	4	3	4	74	
	T53	Rd 4	4	4	4	5	4	5	5	2	4	4	5	4	3	3	5	4	3	3	71	+7 **291**
Kevin Chappell	T51	Rd 1	3	4	4	5	3	4	3	2	4	5	5	3	5	2	3	8	4	4	71	
USA	T67	Rd 2	4	5	5	5	3	5	4	3	4	4	5	4	5	2	5	5	3	4	75	
£16,760	T62	Rd 3	4	4	4	5	4	5	4	3	4	6	4	3	5	4	3	4	3	4	73	
	T53	Rd 4	4	3	4	5	4	6	4	3	6	4	5	4	4	2	3	4	3	4	72	+7 **291**
KT Kim	T35	Rd 1	3	5	4	5	3	5	3	3	4	4	4	3	4	3	4	5	4	4	70	
Korea	T22	Rd 2	4	4	3	5	3	6	5	3	5	4	4	4	3	3	4	4	3	4	71	
£16,760	T50	Rd 3	4	5	4	4	3	5	5	3	4	5	4	5	4	3	4	5	3	7	77	
	T53	Rd 4	4	4	4	4	3	4	4	3	4	5	6	4	5	3	4	5	3	4	73	+7 **291**
Marc Leishman	T110	Rd 1	3	5	3	4	3	5	4	3	6	4	4	4	5	3	6	5	3	4	74	
Australia	T41	Rd 2	4	4	4	4	3	4	4	3	4	4	4	4	4	3	4	5	3	4	69	
£16,760	T50	Rd 3	4	4	4	5	4	4	4	6	5	4	4	4	3	4	5	5	3	4	75	
	T53	Rd 4	5	4	4	4	3	5	4	3	4	5	5	4	4	2	5	5	3	4	73	+7 **291**
Justin Thomas	T4	Rd 1	3	3	3	4	3	5	3	3	4	5	4	4	3	3	6	5	3	3	67	
USA	T50	Rd 2	4	5	4	5	4	5	4	3	6	4	5	5	4	3	5	4	3	4	77	
£16,760	T50	Rd 3	4	4	5	4	4	5	4	3	4	4	4	4	4	3	4	5	5	4	74	
	T53	Rd 4	4	5	4	4	4	4	4	4	4	5	4	4	4	2	4	4	3	5	73	+7 **291**

HOLE			1	2	3	4	5	6	7	8	9	10	11	12	13	14	15	16	17	18		
PAR	POS		4	4	4	4	5	4	4	3	4	4	3	4	4	5	4	4	4	4		TOTAL
Ryan Evans	T51	Rd 1	4	4	4	5	3	5	4	2	4	3	4	4	4	4	5	5	3	4	71	
England	T67	Rd 2	4	5	4	5	4	5	4	3	4	4	4	5	4	3	5	4	3	5	75	
£16,200	T65	Rd 3	3	4	4	5	4	6	3	4	3	4	4	4	5	3	5	6	3	4	74	
	58	Rd 4	4	4	4	4	3	4	4	4	4	4	4	4	5	3	4	5	4	4	72	+8 **292**
Daniel Summerhays	T51	Rd 1	4	5	4	4	3	5	4	3	3	4	4	4	4	3	4	5	4	4	71	
USA	T50	Rd 2	5	4	4	6	2	5	4	3	5	4	6	4	3	3	4	4	3	4	73	
£15,950	T73	Rd 3	4	4	4	6	3	5	4	4	4	5	4	4	5	3	5	5	4	4	77	
	T59	Rd 4	3	5	3	5	4	6	3	3	4	4	4	5	4	3	4	5	3	4	72	+9 **293**
Jon Rahm	T110	Rd 1	4	4	4	5	3	6	5	3	4	4	4	4	4	4	5	4	3	4	74	
Spain	T58	Rd 2	5	5	5	5	2	4	4	3	5	4	4	4	4	2	4	4	3	4	71	
£15,950	T50	Rd 3	3	4	3	5	3	4	5	3	4	7	5	5	4	3	4	4	3	4	73	
	T59	Rd 4	5	4	4	5	3	5	3	4	4	5	6	4	4	3	4	4	4	4	75	+9 **293**
Jim Furyk	T110	Rd 1	3	3	4	4	3	5	4	3	4	5	5	4	5	4	5	6	3	4	74	
USA	T67	Rd 2	4	3	4	6	3	5	4	2	4	5	4	4	4	2	5	5	4	4	72	
£15,950	T50	Rd 3	4	4	4	5	3	5	4	3	4	4	4	4	4	3	6	4	3	4	72	
	T59	Rd 4	4	3	4	3	5	5	4	3	4	5	5	5	4	3	5	5	4	4	75	+9 **293**
Byeong Hun An	T35	Rd 1	4	4	4	3	2	5	4	4	3	4	6	4	4	3	4	4	4	4	70	
Korea	T15	Rd 2	4	4	4	5	3	5	4	2	5	4	3	4	4	2	4	4	4	5	70	
£15,950	T39	Rd 3	4	5	3	7	4	5	4	3	4	4	4	4	4	3	4	7	3	4	76	
	T59	Rd 4	4	4	5	5	5	5	3	3	4	4	4	5	4	3	5	7	3	4	77	+9 **293**
Mark O'Meara	T51	Rd 1	3	4	3	6	3	5	4	2	4	4	4	4	4	3	6	5	3	4	71	
USA	T41	Rd 2	4	4	4	6	3	5	4	2	5	4	4	4	4	3	3	5	3	5	72	
£15,600	T73	Rd 3	4	4	4	5	3	7	4	3	4	5	5	4	4	4	5	5	4	4	78	
	T63	Rd 4	4	4	4	4	2	5	3	3	4	4	5	4	5	3	7	5	3	4	73	+10 **294**
Paul Lawrie	T75	Rd 1	4	4	4	4	3	5	5	2	5	4	4	5	4	3	4	5	3	4	72	
Scotland	T67	Rd 2	4	5	5	4	3	5	4	3	4	5	4	5	4	3	5	4	3	4	74	
£15,600	T65	Rd 3	5	5	4	5	3	3	4	3	4	4	4	5	4	3	5	5	4	4	74	
	T63	Rd 4	4	4	4	5	3	6	4	3	4	4	5	4	5	3	4	5	3	4	74	+10 **294**
Graeme McDowell	T122	Rd 1	3	5	4	5	3	5	4	4	4	6	5	4	4	3	4	5	3	4	75	
Northern Ireand	T67	Rd 2	4	3	3	5	3	4	3	3	4	5	4	4	4	3	6	5	4	4	71	
£15,600	T50	Rd 3	3	4	4	5	3	5	4	6	4	4	4	4	3	4	4	4	3	4	72	
	T63	Rd 4	5	5	3	5	3	5	4	4	6	4	3	4	5	4	4	5	3	4	76	+10 **294**
Zander Lombard	T22	Rd 1	4	3	5	4	3	5	4	2	4	4	5	4	4	3	4	4	3	4	69	
South Africa	T58	Rd 2	4	7	4	5	5	5	4	3	4	4	4	4	4	2	5	5	3	4	76	
£15,350	T62	Rd 3	4	3	4	5	3	5	4	3	4	5	5	5	5	3	5	4	3	4	74	
	T66	Rd 4	4	4	3	4	3	5	5	3	5	4	7	4	4	4	5	5	3	4	76	+11 **295**
Harold Varner III	T51	Rd 1	4	4	4	5	3	4	4	3	4	4	4	4	4	3	4	5	3	5	71	
USA	T41	Rd 2	4	4	4	5	3	5	4	3	4	5	4	4	4	3	4	5	3	4	72	
£15,350	T50	Rd 3	4	4	4	4	3	5	4	3	4	6	4	5	4	3	4	6	4	4	75	
	T66	Rd 4	4	5	4	4	3	5	3	3	4	4	5	7	5	4	4	6	3	4	77	+11 **295**
Marco Dawson	T75	Rd 1	4	3	4	5	3	4	4	3	4	5	5	4	4	2	5	5	4	4	72	
USA	T58	Rd 2	4	4	4	5	3	6	5	2	4	5	3	5	4	3	4	5	3	4	73	
£15,050	T77	Rd 3	4	5	4	4	3	5	4	3	4	6	5	4	4	3	6	5	4	4	77	
	T68	Rd 4	4	6	4	4	3	5	4	3	4	4	5	4	5	3	4	5	3	4	74	+12 **296**
Patton Kizzire	T134	Rd 1	4	4	3	6	3	4	5	3	4	4	5	4	4	4	5	5	5	4	76	
USA	T67	Rd 2	4	3	4	6	3	5	4	3	4	4	4	4	2	4	4	4	4	4	70	
£15,050	T73	Rd 3	4	4	3	5	3	6	4	3	4	6	4	5	6	3	4	4	3	4	75	
	T68	Rd 4	4	4	3	5	3	5	4	3	4	5	6	4	4	3	5	5	3	5	75	+12 **296**

HOLE			1	2	3	4	5	6	7	8	9	10	11	12	13	14	15	16	17	18	
PAR	POS		4	4	4	4	5	4	4	3	4	4	3	4	4	5	4	4	4	4	TOTAL
James Hahn	T110	Rd 1	4	4	4	4	4	5	4	3	4	4	4	5	4	3	4	7	3	4	74
USA	T67	Rd 2	5	4	4	5	4	6	4	3	4	4	3	4	3	2	4	6	3	4	72
£15,050	T65	Rd 3	4	4	4	5	3	5	4	3	4	4	4	5	5	3	5	4	3	5	74
	T68	Rd 4	5	4	4	5	3	5	3	4	4	4	5	5	5	3	5	5	3	4	76 +12 **296**
Anirban Lahiri	T22	Rd 1	4	3	4	4	4	5	3	3	4	4	4	4	4	3	4	5	3	4	69
India	T22	Rd 2	4	4	4	6	3	5	4	2	5	5	4	4	4	3	4	4	3	4	72
£15,050	T43	Rd 3	4	6	4	4	3	5	4	3	4	5	5	5	4	3	4	5	3	5	76
	T68	Rd 4	5	4	4	6	3	6	5	3	4	4	4	4	4	3	5	5	4	6	79 +12 **296**
Scott Hend	T51	Rd 1	4	4	4	5	3	5	3	2	4	4	4	4	5	3	4	7	3	3	71
Australia	T50	Rd 2	3	4	3	4	3	4	4	4	4	6	4	3	5	3	5	5	5	4	73
£14,650	T73	Rd 3	3	4	3	5	3	6	5	3	4	5	5	4	5	3	7	3	3	4	77
	T72	Rd 4	5	4	4	4	4	4	4	6	4	4	4	5	4	3	5	5	3	4	76 +13 **297**
Yuta Ikeda	T12	Rd 1	4	4	4	4	3	4	4	4	3	4	4	4	4	2	4	5	3	4	68
Japan	T27	Rd 2	4	4	4	5	4	5	4	3	4	4	4	5	5	3	4	5	3	4	74
£14,650	T65	Rd 3	4	4	4	5	5	6	4	2	5	4	6	4	4	3	5	6	3	4	78
	T72	Rd 4	6	5	3	5	4	5	3	5	5	3	5	4	4	4	5	4	3	4	77 +13 **297**
Branden Grace	T35	Rd 1	4	4	4	5	3	5	3	2	4	5	4	4	4	3	4	5	3	4	70
South Africa	T50	Rd 2	4	5	4	5	3	5	5	3	4	4	6	4	5	3	3	4	3	4	74
£14,650	T65	Rd 3	4	4	3	5	4	4	4	4	4	5	4	5	5	2	6	6	3	4	76
	T72	Rd 4	5	3	4	5	4	5	4	3	4	4	5	4	4	4	5	5	3	6	77 +13 **297**
Jamie Donaldson	T22	Rd 1	4	4	4	4	3	4	4	3	4	4	4	4	5	3	4	5	2	4	69
Wales	T27	Rd 2	4	4	4	5	3	5	4	3	5	4	4	5	3	3	4	5	3	5	73
£14,650	T50	Rd 3	4	5	4	5	3	5	3	4	4	5	5	5	4	3	5	5	3	4	76
	T72	Rd 4	4	4	4	5	4	7	4	2	4	4	5	8	4	4	4	5	3	4	79 +13 **297**
Kevin Kisner	T35	Rd 1	3	4	4	4	3	5	4	2	5	5	3	6	4	3	3	5	3	5	70
USA	T27	Rd 2	3	4	5	5	3	5	5	3	4	4	4	4	3	4	5	5	3	4	72
£14,400	T77	Rd 3	4	4	5	5	5	5	4	3	5	5	4	4	5	2	5	5	3	7	80
	76	Rd 4	5	4	4	4	3	5	4	3	5	4	4	5	5	4	5	5	3	4	76 +14 **298**
Charley Hoffman	T51	Rd 1	4	4	4	5	2	6	4	3	4	4	5	4	4	3	3	5	3	4	71
USA	T50	Rd 2	5	4	4	4	3	5	3	3	5	4	4	4	4	3	4	5	4	5	73
£14,300	T77	Rd 3	4	5	5	4	4	5	4	2	4	4	8	4	5	2	4	6	4	4	78
	77	Rd 4	4	5	4	5	4	5	4	3	4	4	4	5	4	3	6	5	4	4	77 +15 **299**
Colin Montgomerie	T51	Rd 1	6	4	3	4	3	4	4	2	3	4	5	4	4	4	4	6	3	4	71
Scotland	T67	Rd 2	4	4	4	5	3	5	4	3	4	4	6	4	4	3	5	5	3	5	75
£14,200	81	Rd 3	4	5	4	5	2	6	4	3	5	6	3	4	5	4	6	5	3	5	79
	78	Rd 4	4	5	4	6	3	6	4	2	5	4	5	5	4	3	4	5	3	4	76 +17 **301**
Kodai Ichihara	T22	Rd 1	4	4	4	4	3	5	3	3	5	5	4	3	3	2	4	6	3	4	69
Japan	T67	Rd 2	5	5	5	5	4	4	4	4	5	4	5	5	3	2	5	5	3	4	77
£14,050	80	Rd 3	5	4	4	4	2	5	5	4	4	6	8	4	4	3	5	5	3	3	78
	T79	Rd 4	4	5	4	5	3	5	4	3	6	4	4	5	5	3	5	5	3	5	78 +18 **302**
Soomin Lee	T12	Rd 1	4	4	4	4	3	4	3	2	4	4	4	4	4	3	4	6	3	4	68
Korea	T58	Rd 2	5	5	4	5	4	6	4	3	5	4	3	5	5	3	5	5	3	3	77
£14,050	T65	Rd 3	3	6	4	5	3	5	4	3	3	5	4	5	4	3	5	5	3	5	75
	T79	Rd 4	5	5	6	5	4	5	4	4	4	4	5	5	3	3	5	7	4	4	82 +18 **302**
Greg Chalmers	T75	Rd 1	3	4	4	4	4	5	4	2	4	5	6	4	5	2	4	5	2	5	72
Australia	T41	Rd 2	4	4	5	4	3	5	5	2	4	3	4	4	4	3	5	5	3	4	71
£13,900	T65	Rd 3	3	4	4	5	4	4	5	4	4	4	4	4	5	3	5	6	5	4	77
	81	Rd 4	4	5	4	4	3	5	6	5	4	4	8	4	4	3	6	6	4	6	85 +21 **305**

NON QUALIFIERS AFTER 36 HOLES

(Leading 10 professionals and ties receive £4,625 each, next 20 professionals and ties receive £3,700 each, remainder of professionals receive £3,100 each.)

HOLE			1	2	3	4	5	6	7	8	9	10	11	12	13	14	15	16	17	18	
PAR	POS		4	4	4	4	5	4	4	3	4	4	3	4	4	5	4	4	4	4	TOTAL
Robert Streb	T110	Rd 1	3	4	4	4	3	6	5	3	5	4	4	5	5	3	4	5	3	4	74
USA	**T82**	Rd 2	4	4	4	5	2	6	3	3	5	4	4	5	4	3	4	5	4	4	73 +5 **147**
Ernie Els	T51	Rd 1	4	5	3	4	2	6	3	3	4	4	6	4	4	2	4	6	3	4	71
South Africa	**T82**	Rd 2	5	4	4	7	2	5	3	2	6	5	4	4	4	3	6	4	3	5	76 +5 **147**
Marcus Fraser	T75	Rd 1	4	4	3	5	3	5	4	2	3	6	5	4	5	2	4	5	3	5	72
Australia	**T82**	Rd 2	4	4	4	5	3	6	4	3	4	4	4	4	5	3	6	5	3	4	75 +5 **147**
Richie Ramsay	T94	Rd 1	4	4	4	4	3	5	4	3	4	4	5	4	4	4	5	5	3	4	73
Scotland	**T82**	Rd 2	4	5	3	5	3	5	4	3	4	4	6	5	4	3	4	5	3	4	74 +5 **147**
George Coetzee	T122	Rd 1	4	4	4	4	3	5	4	3	6	4	5	4	4	4	4	4	4	5	75
South Africa	**T82**	Rd 2	4	4	4	5	3	5	4	3	5	4	4	5	4	3	4	4	3	4	72 +5 **147**
William McGirt	T122	Rd 1	5	4	5	4	3	5	4	3	4	5	6	5	4	4	4	4	3	3	75
USA	**T82**	Rd 2	4	3	6	4	3	5	4	3	3	5	5	4	4	3	4	4	4	4	72 +5 **147**
Rod Pampling	T75	Rd 1	4	5	4	5	3	4	4	2	4	5	5	4	4	3	3	5	3	5	72
Australia	**T82**	Rd 2	3	4	4	5	3	5	4	5	4	5	4	4	3	3	5	5	4	5	75 +5 **147**
Jordan Niebrugge	T75	Rd 1	4	4	3	6	4	4	4	4	3	4	5	4	4	4	4	4	3	4	72
USA	**T89**	Rd 2	5	4	4	5	3	5	4	3	5	5	4	6	4	3	4	5	3	4	76 +6 **148**
Todd Hamilton	T122	Rd 1	4	5	4	4	3	5	4	3	4	4	5	4	4	3	5	5	4	5	75
USA	**T89**	Rd 2	4	4	4	4	4	5	3	3	4	4	4	3	5	5	4	5	4	4	73 +6 **148**
Justin Leonard	T35	Rd 1	4	4	4	4	3	5	4	2	3	4	3	4	4	4	5	4	4	5	70
USA	**T89**	Rd 2	4	4	4	5	4	5	5	2	4	4	4	5	5	5	7	4	4	3	78 +6 **148**
Mark Calcavecchia	T94	Rd 1	5	4	3	6	4	5	4	3	4	4	3	4	4	3	4	5	3	5	73
USA	**T89**	Rd 2	4	4	3	6	2	4	4	4	4	4	5	5	4	4	5	5	3	5	75 +6 **148**
Steven Alker	T94	Rd 1	4	4	4	5	4	5	4	3	3	5	4	4	4	3	5	5	3	4	73
New Zealand	**T89**	Rd 2	4	4	4	5	4	5	4	2	4	5	4	4	5	3	5	5	4	4	75 +6 **148**
David Lingmerth	T94	Rd 1	3	4	4	4	2	5	5	4	5	4	4	4	4	4	6	5	3	3	73
Sweden	**T89**	Rd 2	3	4	5	4	5	6	4	3	5	4	4	5	2	5	4	5	3	4	75 +6 **148**
Vijay Singh	T22	Rd 1	3	4	3	5	3	4	5	2	4	4	5	5	4	2	4	5	3	4	69
Fiji	**T89**	Rd 2	4	5	4	5	3	6	4	4	3	5	4	6	5	3	6	5	3	4	79 +6 **148**
Smylie Kaufman	T75	Rd 1	5	5	5	4	3	4	4	3	4	4	4	4	4	3	3	5	2	6	72
USA	**T89**	Rd 2	5	4	4	5	3	5	4	6	5	4	5	4	4	3	4	5	3	3	76 +6 **148**
Chris Kirk	T75	Rd 1	3	5	4	7	3	3	4	3	4	4	4	4	4	3	5	5	3	4	72
USA	**T89**	Rd 2	4	4	4	5	4	6	5	3	4	5	5	5	5	2	4	5	2	4	76 +6 **148**
Matteo Manassero	T35	Rd 1	4	4	4	5	3	3	3	5	4	4	7	4	4	2	3	4	3	4	70
Italy	**T89**	Rd 2	4	3	5	5	4	5	4	4	4	6	4	4	5	4	4	6	3	4	78 +6 **148**
Shugo Imahira	T12	Rd 1	4	4	4	4	4	3	4	3	3	4	4	4	4	3	4	5	3	4	68
Japan	**T89**	Rd 2	4	4	6	4	4	5	3	7	5	5	5	6	3	3	5	4	3	4	80 +6 **148**
Nathan Holman	T75	Rd 1	3	5	3	5	3	5	4	5	4	3	5	5	4	4	4	4	3	3	72
Australia	**T89**	Rd 2	5	4	3	5	3	5	5	6	4	4	5	4	4	3	5	4	4	3	76 +6 **148**
Joost Luiten	T122	Rd 1	4	3	4	7	3	5	4	3	4	4	4	5	3	4	4	5	5	4	75
Netherlands	**T101**	Rd 2	4	5	4	4	3	4	5	3	5	5	4	5	4	3	4	5	3	4	74 +7 **149**
Tommy Fleetwood	T94	Rd 1	4	4	4	5	4	5	6	3	4	4	3	4	5	2	4	5	3	4	73
England	**T101**	Rd 2	4	5	4	5	3	7	4	3	5	4	4	5	3	4	5	4	3	4	76 +7 **149**

HOLE			1	2	3	4	5	6	7	8	9	10	11	12	13	14	15	16	17	18			
PAR	POS		4	4	4	4	5	4	4	3	4	4	3	4	4	5	4	4	4	4	TOTAL		
Anthony Wall	T134	Rd 1	4	4	4	5	3	5	5	2	5	4	8	4	4	3	5	5	3	3	76		
England	**T101**	Rd 2	4	3	3	5	3	5	4	3	5	5	4	5	4	3	5	5	3	4	73	+7	**149**
Colt Knost	T110	Rd 1	4	3	4	4	3	5	3	3	4	6	4	4	4	4	4	4	6	5	74		
USA	**T101**	Rd 2	4	5	4	6	4	5	4	3	4	4	5	4	4	4	4	5	3	3	75	+7	**149**
Callum Shinkwin	T94	Rd 1	4	3	4	5	2	5	3	4	4	5	4	4	4	3	5	5	3	6	73		
England	**T101**	Rd 2	3	4	5	4	4	5	4	4	5	4	5	4	4	4	4	4	5	4	76	+7	**149**
Sang-hee Lee	T94	Rd 1	3	3	4	4	3	5	4	3	4	4	5	4	4	3	5	7	4	4	73		
Korea	**T101**	Rd 2	4	4	4	5	3	5	5	3	4	4	4	4	4	4	4	7	3	5	76	+7	**149**
K Aphibarnrat	T122	Rd 1	5	4	4	3	4	4	3	3	4	4	7	4	4	2	6	6	4	4	75		
Thailand	**T101**	Rd 2	5	7	4	3	3	5	4	2	6	5	4	4	2	4	4	4	4	4	74	+7	**149**
Shane Lowry	T148	Rd 1	4	5	4	5	4	5	4	3	3	5	5	6	4	3	4	5	4	5	78		
Republic of Ireland	**T101**	Rd 2	3	3	4	5	3	5	4	3	4	4	4	4	5	3	4	6	3	4	71	+7	**149**
Ross Fisher	T51	Rd 1	3	4	4	4	3	4	3	3	4	5	5	5	4	3	4	5	3	5	71		
England	**T101**	Rd 2	4	4	4	5	4	6	5	3	4	6	4	4	5	3	5	5	3	4	78	+7	**149**
Brendan Steele	T94	Rd 1	4	4	3	4	3	4	5	3	4	7	5	4	4	3	4	5	3	4	73		
USA	**T101**	Rd 2	4	4	5	5	3	5	4	3	4	5	5	4	4	3	4	5	4	5	76	+7	**149**
Clément Sordet	T122	Rd 1	4	4	3	5	3	5	3	5	4	4	4	5	5	2	7	5	3	4	75		
France	**T111**	Rd 2	5	4	5	4	4	5	4	3	4	4	4	4	5	4	4	5	3	4	75	+8	**150**
Nick Cullen	T110	Rd 1	4	3	4	6	3	7	4	3	4	5	4	5	4	2	4	4	4	4	74		
Australia	**T111**	Rd 2	5	5	3	5	3	7	4	3	4	3	3	5	4	3	6	5	4	4	76	+8	**150**
Yusaku Miyazato	T141	Rd 1	4	4	4	4	4	6	3	7	5	4	4	4	3	4	5	4	4	4	77		
Japan	**T111**	Rd 2	4	4	4	7	3	5	4	2	4	4	4	5	5	2	5	4	3	4	73	+8	**150**
Brian Gay	T134	Rd 1	4	5	5	6	3	5	5	2	4	4	4	4	5	3	5	5	3	4	76		
USA	**T111**	Rd 2	4	4	4	6	4	5	4	2	4	5	5	4	4	3	4	5	3	4	74	+8	**150**
Fabian Gomez	T134	Rd 1	4	4	4	6	4	5	4	3	4	5	7	3	5	3	4	4	3	4	76		
Argentina	**T111**	Rd 2	4	4	4	5	3	4	5	3	4	4	4	5	5	3	5	5	3	4	74	+8	**150**
Jeunghun Wang	T122	Rd 1	5	4	4	4	3	6	5	3	4	4	5	4	4	3	4	5	4	4	75		
Korea	**T111**	Rd 2	4	5	4	5	2	5	4	4	4	4	6	5	4	3	4	5	3	4	75	+8	**150**
Victor Dubuisson	T51	Rd 1	4	4	5	4	3	4	4	2	3	6	5	4	4	3	5	5	3	3	71		
France	**T111**	Rd 2	4	5	4	4	4	5	3	3	5	6	5	5	4	4	4	6	3	5	79	+8	**150**
Hideki Matsuyama	T75	Rd 1	3	4	4	4	3	5	4	3	3	5	4	4	5	3	4	5	4	4	72		
Japan	**T111**	Rd 2	4	4	4	5	2	6	4	4	4	5	5	5	4	3	4	6	4	5	78	+8	**150**
Russell Henley	T94	Rd 1	4	5	4	5	3	4	4	4	4	4	4	3	4	3	6	4	4	4	73		
USA	**T111**	Rd 2	5	4	5	4	3	5	4	3	4	6	7	4	4	4	4	5	2	4	77	+8	**150**
Robert Rock	T51	Rd 1	4	4	3	4	3	4	4	3	4	5	4	4	4	3	5	6	3	4	71		
England	**T111**	Rd 2	4	5	5	5	3	6	4	3	4	7	5	3	5	3	5	4	4	4	79	+8	**150**
Dave Coupland	T75	Rd 1	4	3	4	5	3	5	4	3	4	4	4	4	4	5	5	5	2	5	72		
England	**T111**	Rd 2	3	4	5	5	4	5	5	3	6	5	4	4	3	5	5	4	4	4	78	+8	**150**
Kristoffer Broberg	T141	Rd 1	4	4	3	5	4	4	4	4	3	4	9	5	4	3	5	5	3	4	77		
Sweden	**T122**	Rd 2	4	4	5	5	3	5	4	2	4	4	4	4	5	3	4	6	3	5	74	+9	**151**
John Daly	T122	Rd 1	5	4	3	5	3	5	3	3	7	4	5	4	4	3	4	6	3	4	75		
USA	**T122**	Rd 2	4	4	5	5	3	5	4	3	4	5	5	4	4	3	4	6	3	5	76	+9	**151**
Paul Casey	T141	Rd 1	4	4	4	4	3	6	3	4	4	4	6	5	4	3	4	5	5	5	77		
England	**T122**	Rd 2	4	5	3	4	2	5	7	3	5	5	4	4	4	3	4	5	3	4	74	+9	**151**
Bernd Wiesberger	T110	Rd 1	4	5	4	5	4	4	5	4	4	4	4	4	3	4	5	3	4	4	74		
Austria	**T122**	Rd 2	4	4	4	4	3	5	6	3	6	4	6	4	6	3	3	5	3	4	77	+9	**151**

HOLE		1	2	3	4	5	6	7	8	9	10	11	12	13	14	15	16	17	18		
PAR	POS	4	4	4	4	5	4	4	3	4	4	3	4	4	5	4	4	4	4		TOTAL
Brandon Stone T94 Rd 1		4	5	3	4	3	6	5	4	3	4	4	4	5	4	4	4	3	4		73
South Africa **T122** Rd 2		4	5	5	5	2	6	5	2	6	4	5	5	4	3	4	4	4	5		78 +9 **151**
Scott Gregory* T148 Rd 1		3	4	4	4	3	4	4	3	4	3	7	5	7	2	5	6	5	5		78
England **T122** Rd 2		5	4	4	4	2	4	4	3	4	4	4	4	5	3	7	5	3	4		73 +9 **151**
Thorbjørn Olesen T75 Rd 1		4	4	4	5	2	4	3	3	4	5	5	5	4	3	5	5	3	4		72
Denmark **T122** Rd 2		5	7	4	5	4	5	4	2	4	4	3	5	5	4	5	6	3	4		79 +9 **151**
Hideto Tanihara T75 Rd 1		4	4	4	5	4	5	3	3	4	4	5	4	5	3	4	4	3	4		72
Japan **T122** Rd 2		4	4	3	6	4	5	5	4	4	5	5	4	5	3	5	5	4	4		79 +9 **151**
Yosuke Tsukada T110 Rd 1		4	5	4	5	4	4	2	5	5	5	5	4	3	4	3	5	4	4		74
Japan **T130** Rd 2		4	4	5	5	3	6	4	4	5	4	4	5	5	2	4	6	4	4		78 +10 **152**
Jack Senior T152 Rd 1		4	5	4	5	4	6	4	4	5	4	4	5	4	3	5	5	4	4		79
England **T130** Rd 2		3	4	4	5	3	5	3	3	4	5	5	4	4	3	4	5	4	5		73 +10 **152**
James Heath T122 Rd 1		4	4	5	5	3	5	4	6	5	4	4	4	5	3	4	3	3	4		75
England **T130** Rd 2		4	4	5	6	4	4	6	3	5	4	4	3	4	3	6	5	3	4		77 +10 **152**
Jimmy Walker T75 Rd 1		3	4	4	4	2	5	3	4	4	5	5	5	3	7	4	3	4	4		72
USA **T130** Rd 2		3	4	4	5	5	6	4	3	5	4	5	7	4	3	4	6	5	5		80 +10 **152**
Billy Horschel T4 Rd 1		4	4	5	5	2	4	4	2	4	4	4	3	3	4	5	2	4	4		67
USA **T130** Rd 2		4	4	4	5	3	7	4	4	4	5	5	6	7	5	4	5	4	5		85 +10 **152**
P Khongwatmai T51 Rd 1		4	4	4	4	3	5	4	3	4	6	4	4	4	3	4	4	3	4		71
Thailand **T130** Rd 2		4	5	5	4	4	5	5	3	4	4	6	4	4	3	8	5	4	4		81 +10 **152**
Scott Fernandez T75 Rd 1		4	4	3	4	3	5	5	3	4	5	4	5	4	3	4	5	3	4		72
Spain **T130** Rd 2		4	5	5	5	4	5	4	3	4	4	6	5	5	3	5	5	3	5		80 +10 **152**
Rikard Karlberg T110 Rd 1		4	4	4	6	3	5	5	3	4	5	4	4	3	4	4	5	3	4		74
Sweden **T130** Rd 2		4	4	5	5	4	5	3	5	7	5	3	4	4	3	4	6	3	4		78 +10 **152**
Seung Yul Noh T122 Rd 1		4	4	4	5	3	7	4	2	4	4	6	5	5	2	4	5	3	4		75
Korea **T138** Rd 2		4	5	4	5	4	4	3	7	4	4	5	4	3	4	5	5	3	5		78 +11 **153**
Lasse Jensen T148 Rd 1		5	5	4	5	3	5	4	3	6	4	5	4	4	4	4	5	3	5		78
Denmark **T138** Rd 2		4	5	4	6	3	6	4	3	3	4	4	5	4	3	5	5	3	4		75 +11 **153**
Satoshi Kodaira T134 Rd 1		4	5	4	5	3	5	4	3	4	4	4	3	5	5	5	6	3	4		76
Japan **T138** Rd 2		4	3	5	6	3	6	4	2	5	4	4	4	3	5	5	4	4	6		77 +11 **153**
Marc Warren T141 Rd 1		3	4	6	3	2	5	4	3	4	4	5	5	4	3	5	5	5	5		77
Scotland **T138** Rd 2		4	3	4	4	3	5	5	3	6	4	4	5	4	4	4	7	3	4		76 +11 **153**
Matthew Fitzpatrick T94 Rd 1		4	4	5	5	3	4	4	3	3	4	7	4	4	3	4	5	3	4		73
England **T138** Rd 2		4	4	4	5	3	6	5	3	4	4	5	5	5	3	6	5	3	6		80 +11 **153**
Stefano Mazzoli* T134 Rd 1		4	4	4	4	3	5	4	2	5	4	7	4	6	4	3	5	3	5		76
Italy **T143** Rd 2		6	4	4	5	4	7	5	3	5	4	3	4	6	2	5	4	3	4		78 +12 **154**
Paul Howard T94 Rd 1		4	4	4	4	3	4	5	3	4	5	7	5	4	2	5	4	3	3		73
England **T143** Rd 2		4	4	4	5	3	4	4	4	5	4	7	7	4	3	4	6	4	5		81 +12 **154**
Louis Oosthuizen T51 Rd 1		4	4	4	5	3	5	4	4	4	5	4	4	4	1	4	5	3	4		71
South Africa **T143** Rd 2		4	4	4	5	3	6	5	3	4	5	9	4	5	4	4	7	3	4		83 +12 **154**
James Morrison T134 Rd 1		4	6	4	5	4	4	4	3	4	4	4	4	3	5	5	5	4	5		76
England **T143** Rd 2		4	5	5	5	4	5	5	5	4	4	4	4	5	3	4	5	3	4		78 +12 **154**
Danny Lee T148 Rd 1		3	6	4	5	3	4	4	3	3	5	7	5	5	3	5	5	4	5		78
New Zealand **T147** Rd 2		5	4	5	5	3	4	5	4	4	5	4	5	4	3	3	5	4	5		77 +13 **155**
Paul Dunne T141 Rd 1		4	4	4	4	3	6	3	3	4	4	5	4	6	4	5	5	4	5		77
Republic of Ireland **T147** Rd 2		4	4	4	6	5	6	4	4	5	4	4	4	3	3	4	7	4	3		78 +13 **155**

HOLE			1	2	3	4	5	6	7	8	9	10	11	12	13	14	15	16	17	18		
PAR	POS		4	4	4	4	5	4	4	3	4	4	3	4	4	5	4	4	4	4	TOTAL	
Jamie Lovemark	T110	Rd 1	4	4	3	5	3	5	3	3	4	5	7	3	4	3	5	6	3	4	74	
USA	**T147**	Rd 2	5	4	6	5	3	5	5	2	5	4	4	9	4	4	4	5	3	4	81 +13	**155**
Steven Bowditch	T152	Rd 1	3	4	4	5	3	5	5	3	4	5	9	4	6	3	4	5	3	4	79	
Australia	**150**	Rd 2	4	4	4	5	4	5	5	2	4	5	5	4	5	4	4	5	4	5	78 +15	**157**
Scott Piercy	T141	Rd 1	4	4	4	4	5	4	4	3	4	4	2	4	6	6	5	5	5	4	77	
USA	**151**	Rd 2	6	5	4	5	3	6	4	3	4	5	4	4	8	3	4	5	4	4	81 +16	**158**
Oskar Arvidsson	T122	Rd 1	5	5	3	4	3	5	4	3	5	5	4	5	4	4	4	5	4	3	75	
Sweden	**152**	Rd 2	4	5	4	5	4	7	4	3	5	5	6	5	4	4	5	6	4	4	84 +17	**159**
Ben Curtis	T141	Rd 1	4	5	4	5	3	6	4	3	4	8	4	5	4	2	5	5	3	3	77	
USA	**153**	Rd 2	4	4	10	5	4	5	5	3	5	5	5	4	4	3	5	5	4	3	83 +18	**160**
Sandy Lyle	155	Rd 1	5	5	4	6	2	6	5	4	4	4	7	4	6	3	5	6	4	5	85	
Scotland	**154**	Rd 2	5	5	4	6	4	4	4	3	4	6	4	5	4	3	4	4	3	6	78 +21	**163**
David Duval	154	Rd 1	4	4	4	5	2	5	4	4	4	5	9	4	4	4	6	7	3	4	82	
USA																						**WD**
Chris Wood		Rd 1	4	3	5	6	3	5	4	4	4	4	4	5								
England																						**WD**

THE TOP TENS

Driving Distance

1 JB Holmes 311.6
2 Jason Day 310.6
2 Nicolas Colsaerts 310.6
4 Dustin Johnson 309.5
5 Bubba Watson 308.1
6 Tony Finau 304.6
7 Zander Lombard 301.6
8 Adam Scott 300.4
9 Rory McIlroy 299.3
10 Thomas Pieters 298.9
11 Henrik Stenson 296.9

Fairways Hit

Maximum of 56

1 **Emiliano Grillo** **44**
2 Russell Knox 43
3 Søren Kjeldsen 42
3 Alex Noren 42
5 Henrik Stenson 41
6 Steve Stricker 40
6 Andrew Johnston 40
6 Lee Westwood 40
6 KT Kim 40
6 Graeme McDowell 40

Greens in Regulation

Maximum of 72

1 Henrik Stenson 56
2 Dustin Johnson 54
3 Phil Mickelson 53
3 Emiliano Grillo 53
5 Jason Dufner 51
5 Justin Rose 51
7 Adam Scott 50
8 Russell Knox 49
8 Francesco Molinari 49
10 Andy Sullivan 48
10 Ryan Palmer 48
10 Martin Kaymer 48
10 Matt Kuchar 48
10 KT Kim 48
10 Marc Leishman 48

Putts

1 **Steve Stricker** **108**
1 **Patrick Reed** **108**
1 **Brandt Snedeker** **108**
4 Henrik Stenson 110
4 Phil Mickelson 110
4 Tyrrell Hatton 110
4 Richard Sterne 110
4 Kevin Chappell 110
4 Zander Lombard 110
10 JB Holmes 111
10 Zach Johnson 111
10 Tony Finau 111
10 Scott Hend 111
10 Greg Chalmers 111

Statistical Rankings

	Driving Distance	Rank	Fairways Hit	Rank	Greens In Regulation	Rank	Putts	Rank
Byeong Hun An	293.6	20	35	36	41	52	119	48
Keegan Bradley	296.6	12	35	36	47	16	118	43
Rafa Cabrera Bello	290.6	26	38	15	47	16	122	66
Greg Chalmers	282.1	49	29	74	29	81	111	10
Kevin Chappell	284.8	38	31	62	36	73	110	4
Darren Clarke	279.3	52	36	28	45	30	120	55
Nicolas Colsaerts	310.6	2	31	62	43	40	116	33
Marco Dawson	253.4	81	31	62	38	65	115	27
Jason Day	310.6	2	26	78	41	52	114	22
Luke Donald	276.9	56	35	36	39	60	117	37
Jamie Donaldson	283.1	46	37	23	46	26	126	81
Jason Dufner	280.5	51	36	28	51	5	122	66
Harris English	288.6	30	38	15	41	52	119	48
Ryan Evans	296.3	13	27	76	44	36	122	66
Tony Finau	304.6	6	33	52	42	47	111	10
Rickie Fowler	272.1	65	37	23	37	71	112	15
Jim Furyk	263.3	77	37	23	38	65	117	37
Sergio Garcia	294.1	17	36	28	45	30	114	22
Branden Grace	290.8	24	29	74	38	65	118	43
Emiliano Grillo	287.5	32	44	1	53	3	124	74
Bill Haas	295.3	16	38	15	43	40	112	15
James Hahn	271.5	66	36	28	38	65	117	37
Padraig Harrington	286.5	34	31	62	41	52	116	33
Tyrrell Hatton	283.4	45	39	11	44	36	110	4
Scott Hend	291.0	23	22	81	35	75	111	10
Jim Herman	271.0	67	39	11	47	16	121	59
Charley Hoffman	283.9	42	24	80	40	58	124	74
JB Holmes	311.6	1	27	76	47	16	111	10
David Howell	260.9	78	38	15	45	30	118	43
Kodai Ichihara	274.0	64	30	68	34	78	120	55
Yuta Ikeda	284.6	39	32	58	35	75	119	48
Thongchai Jaidee	268.9	71	38	15	47	16	120	55
Miguel Angel Jiménez	265.6	74	39	11	46	26	118	43
Dustin Johnson	309.5	4	32	58	54	2	122	66
Zach Johnson	269.9	68	34	46	42	47	111	10
Andrew Johnston	294.1	17	40	6	47	16	112	15
Matt Jones	286.3	35	38	15	40	58	112	15
Martin Kaymer	285.9	36	33	52	48	10	121	59
KT Kim	274.3	62	40	6	48	10	124	74
Kevin Kisner	275.1	60	34	46	34	78	115	27
Patton Kizzire	287.0	33	35	36	39	60	116	33

	Driving Distance	Rank	Fairways Hit	Rank	Greens In Regulation	Rank	Putts	Rank
Søren Kjeldsen	263.5	76	42	3	46	26	112	15
Russell Knox	282.6	47	43	2	49	8	121	59
Matt Kuchar	269.3	70	36	28	48	10	121	59
Anirban Lahiri	289.5	29	33	52	43	40	124	74
Paul Lawrie	283.9	42	30	68	41	52	122	66
Soomin Lee	276.1	58	34	46	36	73	119	48
Marc Leishman	284.0	41	37	23	48	10	121	59
Zander Lombard	301.6	7	31	62	34	78	110	4
Graeme Mcdowell	266.4	73	40	6	45	30	123	73
Rory McIlroy	299.3	9	36	28	47	16	117	37
Phil Mickelson	274.1	63	38	15	53	3	110	4
Francesco Molinari	274.6	61	39	11	49	8	121	59
Colin Montgomerie	258.5	79	35	36	38	65	120	55
Ryan Moore	263.8	75	35	36	39	60	114	22
Kevin Na	279.3	52	35	36	46	26	112	15
Alex Noren	279.1	54	42	3	41	52	117	37
Mark O'Meara	255.8	80	38	15	37	71	117	37
Ryan Palmer	289.6	28	36	28	48	10	119	48
Thomas Pieters	298.9	10	30	68	45	30	115	27
Haydn Porteous	295.5	15	26	78	42	47	116	33
Jon Rahm	284.4	40	35	36	47	16	124	74
Patrick Reed	295.8	14	31	62	38	65	108	1
Justin Rose	294.0	19	30	68	51	5	122	66
Charl Schwartzel	293.4	21	35	36	47	16	115	27
Adam Scott	300.4	8	33	52	50	7	125	79
Webb Simpson	269.8	69	30	68	43	40	115	27
Brandt Snedeker	275.9	59	33	52	39	60	108	1
Matthew Southgate	283.8	44	37	23	47	16	121	59
Jordan Spieth	289.9	27	32	58	44	36	119	48
Henrik Stenson	296.9	11	41	5	56	1	110	4
Richard Sterne	292.1	22	35	36	35	75	110	4
Steve Stricker	267.0	72	40	6	43	40	108	1
Andy Sullivan	280.9	50	34	46	48	10	115	27
Daniel Summerhays	276.6	57	32	58	42	47	122	66
Justin Thomas	278.9	55	30	68	43	40	118	43
Harold Varner III	290.8	24	33	52	45	30	125	79
Bubba Watson	308.1	5	36	28	44	36	119	48
Lee Westwood	287.6	31	40	6	42	47	114	22
Danny Willett	285.1	37	34	46	39	60	114	22
Gary Woodland	282.3	48	34	46	43	40	112	15

	Driving Distance	Rank	Fairways Hit	Rank	Greens In Regulation	Rank	Putts	Rank
Steven Alker	271.0	126	22	6	19	97	61	104
Kiradech Aphibarnrat	291.5	41	13	137	20	78	55	16
Oskar Arvidsson	273.3	119	9	154	16	145	65	143
Steven Bowditch	293.8	31	17	76	17	133	60	89
Kristoffer Broberg	294.8	27	17	76	20	78	60	89
Mark Calcavecchia	272.5	122	21	10	19	97	56	22
Paul Casey	259.0	147	19	31	26	13	68	153
George Coetzee	298.0	18	14	124	17	133	58	52
Dave Coupland	253.0	151	18	48	18	116	59	70
Nick Cullen	292.3	38	15	113	24	24	62	114
Ben Curtis	261.5	143	16	100	18	116	62	114
John Daly	292.0	39	20	20	18	116	59	70
Victor Dubuisson	292.0	39	16	100	20	78	60	89
Paul Dunne	286.0	64	14	124	20	78	68	153
Ernie Els	291.3	42	16	100	23	35	60	89
Scott Fernandez	301.0	14	14	124	19	97	65	143
Ross Fisher	296.8	19	17	76	19	97	62	114
Matthew Fitzpatrick	275.3	112	23	2	21	60	61	104
Tommy Fleetwood	279.0	97	15	113	19	97	60	89
Marcus Fraser	243.5	154	18	48	21	60	60	89
Brian Gay	257.5	148	12	148	15	148	56	22
Fabian Gomez	261.3	144	16	100	19	97	60	89
Scott Gregory*	283.5	79	17	76	21	60	60	89
Todd Hamilton	272.8	121	18	48	22	46	63	129
James Heath	295.5	22	23	2	24	24	63	129
Russell Henley	278.3	100	17	76	22	46	62	114
Nathan Holman	286.8	58	18	48	21	60	58	52
Billy Horschel	267.0	138	13	137	18	116	58	52
Paul Howard	279.8	92	18	48	17	133	57	39
Shugo Imahira	282.3	84	18	48	17	133	53	4
Lasse Jensen	285.0	69	20	20	22	46	67	152
Rikard Karlberg	290.0	48	13	137	19	97	62	114
Smylie Kaufman	296.0	20	12	148	18	116	58	52
Phachara Khongwatmai	274.0	118	17	76	17	133	58	52
Chris Kirk	265.3	140	18	48	21	60	61	104
Colt Knost	247.3	153	21	10	17	133	56	22
Satoshi Kodaira	279.5	94	18	48	17	133	63	129
Sang-hee Lee	280.0	91	18	48	14	153	55	16
Danny Lee	275.5	110	13	137	16	145	62	114
Justin Leonard	272.0	124	21	10	21	60	60	89
David Lingmerth	268.5	131	15	113	20	78	58	52
Jamie Lovemark	290.8	45	13	137	21	60	63	129
Shane Lowry	283.5	79	11	151	15	148	56	22
Joost Luiten	292.5	36	17	76	21	60	60	89
Sandy Lyle	281.0	87	17	76	15	148	65	143
Matteo Manassero	280.3	90	17	76	21	60	58	52
Hideki Matsuyama	265.3	140	21	10	18	116	59	70
Stefano Mazzoli*	298.5	16	15	113	15	148	55	16
William McGirt	278.8	98	15	113	18	116	56	22
Yusaku Miyazato	287.0	55	23	2	17	133	59	70
James Morrison	268.3	135	16	100	14	153	59	70
Jordan Niebrugge	295.5	22	14	124	18	116	56	22
Seung Yul Noh	291.3	42	15	113	22	46	64	139
Thorbjørn Olesen	284.8	71	18	48	21	60	61	104
Louis Oosthuizen	271.8	125	17	76	20	78	63	129
Rod Pampling	280.8	88	14	124	15	148	54	9
Scott Piercy	286.8	58	14	124	19	97	63	129
Richie Ramsay	276.5	106	18	48	20	78	59	70
Robert Rock	279.3	95	17	76	20	78	62	114
Jack Senior	274.8	115	11	151	17	133	60	89
Callum Shinkwin	303.3	10	13	137	17	133	56	22
Vijay Singh	278.3	100	15	113	19	97	59	70
Clément Sordet	292.8	35	14	124	23	35	65	143
Brendan Steele	285.3	68	17	76	16	145	59	70
Brandon Stone	271.0	126	11	151	17	133	59	70
Robert Streb	289.5	49	14	124	18	116	57	39
Hideto Tanihara	278.5	99	21	10	18	116	63	129
Yosuke Tsukada	277.0	104	16	100	18	116	63	129
Jimmy Walker	277.5	103	14	124	21	60	64	139
Anthony Wall	268.5	131	19	31	22	46	60	89
Jeunghun Wang	279.3	95	16	100	21	60	65	143
Marc Warren	301.3	13	19	31	20	78	65	143
Bernd Wiesberger	275.5	110	21	10	19	97	59	70

Roll of Honour

Year	Champion	Score	Margin	Runners-up	Venue
1860	Willie Park Sr	174	2	Tom Morris Sr	Prestwick
1861	Tom Morris Sr	163	4	Willie Park Sr	Prestwick
1862	Tom Morris Sr	163	13	Willie Park Sr	Prestwick
1863	Willie Park Sr	168	2	Tom Morris Sr	Prestwick
1864	Tom Morris Sr	167	2	Andrew Strath	Prestwick
1865	Andrew Strath	162	2	Willie Park Sr	Prestwick
1866	Willie Park Sr	169	2	David Park	Prestwick
1867	Tom Morris Sr	170	2	Willie Park Sr	Prestwick
1868	Tommy Morris Jr	154	3	Tom Morris Sr	Prestwick
1869	Tommy Morris Jr	157	11	Bob Kirk	Prestwick
1870	Tommy Morris Jr	149	12	Bob Kirk, Davie Strath	Prestwick
1871	*No Competition*				
1872	Tommy Morris Jr	166	3	Davie Strath	Prestwick
1873	Tom Kidd	179	1	Jamie Anderson	St Andrews
1874	Mungo Park	159	2	Tommy Morris Jr	Musselburgh
1875	Willie Park Sr	166	2	Bob Martin	Prestwick
1876	Bob Martin	176	—	Davie Strath	St Andrews
	(Martin was awarded the title when Strath refused to play-off)				
1877	Jamie Anderson	160	2	Bob Pringle	Musselburgh
1878	Jamie Anderson	157	2	Bob Kirk	Prestwick
1879	Jamie Anderson	169	3	Jamie Allan, Andrew Kirkaldy	St Andrews
1880	Bob Ferguson	162	5	Peter Paxton	Musselburgh
1881	Bob Ferguson	170	3	Jamie Anderson	Prestwick
1882	Bob Ferguson	171	3	Willie Fernie	St Andrews
1883	Willie Fernie	158	Play-off	Bob Ferguson	Musselburgh
1884	Jack Simpson	160	4	Douglas Rolland, Willie Fernie	Prestwick
1885	Bob Martin	171	1	Archie Simpson	St Andrews
1886	David Brown	157	2	Willie Campbell	Musselburgh
1887	Willie Park Jr	161	1	Bob Martin	Prestwick
1888	Jack Burns	171	1	David Anderson Jr, Ben Sayers	St Andrews
1889	Willie Park Jr	155	Play-off	Andrew Kirkaldy	Musselburgh
1890	John Ball Jr*	164	3	Willie Fernie, Archie Simpson	Prestwick
1891	Hugh Kirkaldy	166	2	Willie Fernie, Andrew Kirkaldy	St Andrews
	(From 1892 the competition was extended to 72 holes)				
1892	Harold Hilton*	305	3 / Sandy Herd	John Ball Jr*, Hugh Kirkaldy,	Muirfield
1893	Willie Auchterlonie	322	2	John Laidlay*	Prestwick

Bobby Locke, 1950

Arnold Palmer, 1962

Tom Weiskopf, 1973

Year	Champion	Score	Margin	Runners-up	Venue
1894	JH Taylor	326	5	Douglas Rolland	St George's
1895	JH Taylor	322	4	Sandy Herd	St Andrews
1896	Harry Vardon	316	Play-off	JH Taylor	Muirfield
1897	Harold Hilton*	314	1	James Braid	Royal Liverpool
1898	Harry Vardon	307	1	Willie Park Jr	Prestwick
1899	Harry Vardon	310	5	Jack White	St George's
1900	JH Taylor	309	8	Harry Vardon	St Andrews
1901	James Braid	309	3	Harry Vardon	Muirfield
1902	Sandy Herd	307	1	Harry Vardon, James Braid	Royal Liverpool
1903	Harry Vardon	300	6	Tom Vardon	Prestwick
1904	Jack White	296	1	James Braid, JH Taylor	Royal St George's
1905	James Braid	318	5	JH Taylor, Rowland Jones	St Andrews
1906	James Braid	300	4	JH Taylor	Muirfield
1907	Arnaud Massy	312	2	JH Taylor	Royal Liverpool
1908	James Braid	291	8	Tom Ball	Prestwick
1909	JH Taylor	295	6	James Braid, Tom Ball	Cinque Ports
1910	James Braid	299	4	Sandy Herd	St Andrews
1911	Harry Vardon	303	Play-off	Arnaud Massy	Royal St George's
1912	Ted Ray	295	4	Harry Vardon	Muirfield
1913	JH Taylor	304	8	Ted Ray	Royal Liverpool
1914	Harry Vardon	306	3	JH Taylor	Prestwick
1915-1919 No Championship					
1920	George Duncan	303	2	Sandy Herd	Royal Cinque Ports
1921	Jock Hutchison	296	Play-off	Roger Wethered*	St Andrews
1922	Walter Hagen	300	1	George Duncan, Jim Barnes	Royal St George's
1923	Arthur Havers	295	1	Walter Hagen	Troon
1924	Walter Hagen	301	1	Ernest Whitcombe	Royal Liverpool
1925	Jim Barnes	300	1	Archie Compston, Ted Ray	Prestwick
1926	Bobby Jones*	291	2	Al Watrous	Royal Lytham
1927	Bobby Jones*	285	6	Aubrey Boomer, Fred Robson	St Andrews
1928	Walter Hagen	292	2	Gene Sarazen	Royal St George's
1929	Walter Hagen	292	6	Johnny Farrell	Muirfield
1930	Bobby Jones*	291	2	Leo Diegel, Macdonald Smith	Royal Liverpool
1931	Tommy Armour	296	1	Jose Jurado	Carnoustie

Year	Champion	Score	Margin	Runners-up	Venue
1932	Gene Sarazen	283	5	Macdonald Smith	Prince's
1933	Denny Shute	292	Play-off	Craig Wood	St Andrews
1934	Henry Cotton	283	5	Sid Brews	Royal St George's
1935	Alf Perry	283	4	Alf Padgham	Muirfield
1936	Alf Padgham	287	1	Jimmy Adams	Royal Liverpool
1937	Henry Cotton	290	2	Reg Whitcombe	Carnoustie
1938	Reg Whitcombe	295	2	Jimmy Adams	Royal St George's
1939	Dick Burton	290	2	Johnny Bulla	St Andrews
1940-1945 No Championship					
1946	Sam Snead	290	4	Bobby Locke, Johnny Bulla	St Andrews
1947	Fred Daly	293	1	Reg Horne, Frank Stranahan*	Royal Liverpool
1948	Henry Cotton	284	5	Fred Daly	Muirfield
1949	Bobby Locke	283	Play-off	Harry Bradshaw	Royal St George's
1950	Bobby Locke	279	2	Roberto de Vicenzo	Troon
1951	Max Faulkner	285	2	Antonio Cerda	Royal Portrush
1952	Bobby Locke	287	1	Peter Thomson	Royal Lytham
1953	Ben Hogan	282	4	Frank Stranahan*, Dai Rees, Peter Thomson, Antonio Cerda	Carnoustie
1954	Peter Thomson	283	1	Syd Scott, Dai Rees, Bobby Locke	Royal Birkdale
1955	Peter Thomson	281	2	John Fallon	St Andrews
1956	Peter Thomson	286	3	Flory Van Donck	Royal Liverpool
1957	Bobby Locke	279	3	Peter Thomson	St Andrews
1958	Peter Thomson	278	Play-off	Dave Thomas	Royal Lytham
1959	Gary Player	284	2	Flory van Donck, Fred Bullock	Muirfield
1960	Kel Nagle	278	1	Arnold Palmer	St Andrews
1961	Arnold Palmer	284	1	Dai Rees	Royal Birkdale
1962	Arnold Palmer	276	6	Kel Nagle	Troon

(Prior to 1963, all holes were played as level 4. From 1963, pars were introduced and holes were played in 3, 4 or 5 shots.)

Year	Champion	To Par	Score	Margin	Runners-up	Venue
1963	Bob Charles	-3	277	Play-off	Phil Rodgers	Royal Lytham
1964	Tony Lema	-9	279	5	Jack Nicklaus	St Andrews
1965	Peter Thomson	-7	285	2	Christy O'Connor Sr, Brian Huggett	Royal Birkdale
1966	Jack Nicklaus	-2	282	1	Dave Thomas, Doug Sanders	Muirfield
1967	Roberto de Vicenzo	-10	278	2	Jack Nicklaus	Royal Liverpool
1968	Gary Player	+1	289	2	Jack Nicklaus, Bob Charles	Carnoustie
1969	Tony Jacklin	-4	280	2	Bob Charles	Royal Lytham
1970	Jack Nicklaus	-5	283	Play-off	Doug Sanders	St Andrews
1971	Lee Trevino	-14	278	1	Liang Huan Lu	Royal Birkdale
1972	Lee Trevino	-6	278	1	Jack Nicklaus	Muirfield
1973	Tom Weiskopf	-12	276	3	Neil Coles, Johnny Miller	Troon
1974	Gary Player	-2	282	4	Peter Oosterhuis	Royal Lytham
1975	Tom Watson	-9	279	Play-off	Jack Newton	Carnoustie
1976	Johnny Miller	-9	279	6	Jack Nicklaus, Seve Ballesteros	Royal Birkdale
1977	Tom Watson	-12	268	1	Jack Nicklaus	Turnberry
1978	Jack Nicklaus	-7	281	2	Simon Owen, Ben Crenshaw, Ray Floyd, Tom Kite	St Andrews
1979	Seve Ballesteros	-1	283	3	Jack Nicklaus, Ben Crenshaw	Royal Lytham
1980	Tom Watson	-13	271	4	Lee Trevino	Muirfield
1981	Bill Rogers	-4	276	4	Bernhard Langer	Royal St George's
1982	Tom Watson	-4	284	1	Peter Oosterhuis, Nick Price	Royal Troon
1983	Tom Watson	-9	275	1	Hale Irwin, Andy Bean	Royal Birkdale
1984	Seve Ballesteros	-12	276	2	Bernhard Langer, Tom Watson	St Andrews

Mark Calcavecchia, 1989 *Justin Leonard, 1997* *Todd Hamilton, 2004*

Year	Champion	To Par	Score	Margin	Runners-up	Venue
1985	Sandy Lyle	+2	282	1	Payne Stewart	Royal St George's
1986	Greg Norman	E	280	5	Gordon J Brand	Turnberry
1987	Nick Faldo	-5	279	1	Rodger Davis, Paul Azinger	Muirfield
1988	Seve Ballesteros	-11	273	2	Nick Price	Royal Lytham
1989	Mark Calcavecchia	-13	275	Play-off	Greg Norman, Wayne Grady	Royal Troon
1990	Nick Faldo	-18	270	5	Mark McNulty, Payne Stewart	St Andrews
1991	Ian Baker-Finch	-8	272	2	Mike Harwood	Royal Birkdale
1992	Nick Faldo	-12	272	1	John Cook	Muirfield
1993	Greg Norman	-13	267	2	Nick Faldo	Royal St George's
1994	Nick Price	-12	268	1	Jesper Parnevik	Turnberry
1995	John Daly	-6	282	Play-off	Costantino Rocca	St Andrews
1996	Tom Lehman	-13	271	2	Mark McCumber, Ernie Els	Royal Lytham
1997	Justin Leonard	-12	272	3	Jesper Parnevik, Darren Clarke	Royal Troon
1998	Mark O'Meara	E	280	Play-off	Brian Watts	Royal Birkdale
1999	Paul Lawrie	+6	290	Play-off	Justin Leonard, Jean Van de Velde	Carnoustie
2000	Tiger Woods	-19	269	8	Ernie Els, Thomas Bjørn	St Andrews
2001	David Duval	-10	274	3	Niclas Fasth	Royal Lytham
2002	Ernie Els	-6	278	Play-off	Thomas Levet, Stuart Appleby, Steve Elkington	Muirfield
2003	Ben Curtis	-1	283	1	Thomas Bjørn, Vijay Singh	Royal St George's
2004	Todd Hamilton	-10	274	Play-off	Ernie Els	Royal Troon
2005	Tiger Woods	-14	274	5	Colin Montgomerie	St Andrews
2006	Tiger Woods	-18	270	2	Chris DiMarco	Royal Liverpool
2007	Padraig Harrington	-7	277	Play-off	Sergio Garcia	Carnoustie
2008	Padraig Harrington	+3	283	4	Ian Poulter	Royal Birkdale
2009	Stewart Cink	-2	278	Play-off	Tom Watson	Turnberry
2010	Louis Oosthuizen	-16	272	7	Lee Westwood	St Andrews
2011	Darren Clarke	-5	275	3	Phil Mickelson, Dustin Johnson	Royal St George's
2012	Ernie Els	-7	273	1	Adam Scott	Royal Lytham
2013	Phil Mickelson	-3	281	3	Henrik Stenson	Muirfield
2014	Rory McIlroy	-17	271	2	Sergio Garcia, Rickie Fowler	Royal Liverpool
2015	Zach Johnson	-15	273	Play-off	Louis Oosthuizen, Marc Leishman	St Andrews
2016	Henrik Stenson	-20	264	3	Phil Mickelson	Royal Troon

Records

Most Victories

6: Harry Vardon, 1896, 1898, 1899, 1903, 1911, 1914
5: James Braid, 1901, 1905, 1906, 1908, 1910; JH Taylor, 1894, 1895, 1900, 1909, 1913; Peter Thomson, 1954, 1955, 1956, 1958, 1965; Tom Watson, 1975, 1977, 1980, 1982, 1983

Most Runner-Up or Joint Runner-Up Finishes

7: Jack Nicklaus, 1964, 1967, 1968, 1972, 1976, 1977, 1979
6: JH Taylor, 1896, 1904, 1905, 1906, 1907, 1914

Oldest Winners

Tom Morris Sr, 1867, 46 years 102 days
Roberto de Vicenzo, 1967, 44 years 92 days
Harry Vardon, 1914, 44 years 41 days
Tom Morris Sr, 1864, 43 years 92 days
Phil Mickelson, 2013, 43 years 35 days
Darren Clarke, 2011, 42 years 337 days
Ernie Els, 2012, 42 years 279 days

Youngest Winners

Tommy Morris Jr, 1868, 17 years 156 days
Tommy Morris Jr, 1869, 18 years 149 days
Tommy Morris Jr, 1870, 19 years 148 days
Willie Auchterlonie, 1893, 21 years 22 days
Tommy Morris Jr, 1872, 21 years 146 days
Seve Ballesteros, 1979, 22 years 103 days

Known Oldest and Youngest Competitors

74 years, 11 months, 24 days: Tom Morris Sr, 1896
74 years, 4 months, 9 days: Gene Sarazen, 1976
14 years, 4 months, 25 days: Tommy Morris Jr, 1865

Largest Margin of Victory

13 strokes, Tom Morris Sr, 1862
12 strokes, Tommy Morris Jr, 1870
11 strokes, Tommy Morris Jr, 1869
8 strokes, JH Taylor, 1900 and 1913; James Braid, 1908; Tiger Woods, 2000

Lowest Winning Total by a Champion

264, Henrik Stenson, Royal Troon, 2016 – 68, 65, 68, 63
267, Greg Norman, Royal St George's, 1993 – 66, 68, 69, 64
268, Tom Watson, Turnberry, 1977 – 68, 70, 65, 65; Nick Price, Turnberry, 1994 – 69, 66, 67, 66

Lowest Total in Relation to Par Since 1963

20 under par: Henrik Stenson, 2016 (264)
19 under par: Tiger Woods, St Andrews, 2000 (269)
18 under par: Nick Faldo, St Andrews, 1990 (270); Tiger Woods, Royal Liverpool, 2006 (270)

Lowest Total by a Runner-Up

267: Phil Mickelson, Royal Troon, 2016 – 63, 69, 70, 65
269: Jack Nicklaus, Turnberry, 1977 – 68, 70, 65, 66; Nick Faldo, Royal St George's, 1993 – 69, 63, 70, 67; Jesper Parnevik, Turnberry, 1994 – 68, 66, 68, 67

Lowest Total by an Amateur

277: Jordan Niebrugge, St Andrews, 2015 – 67, 73, 67, 70

Lowest Individual Round

63: Mark Hayes, second round, Turnberry, 1977; Isao Aoki, third round, Muirfield, 1980; Greg Norman, second round, Turnberry, 1986; Paul Broadhurst, third round, St Andrews, 1990; Jodie Mudd, fourth round, Royal Birkdale, 1991; Nick Faldo, second round, Royal St George's, 1993; Payne Stewart, fourth round, Royal St George's, 1993; Rory McIlroy, first round, St Andrews, 2010; Phil Mickelson, first round, Royal Troon, 2016; Henrik Stenson, fourth round, Royal Troon, 2016

Lowest Individual Round by an Amateur

65: Tom Lewis, first round, Royal St George's, 2011

Lowest First Round

63: Rory McIlroy, St Andrews, 2010; Phil Mickelson, Royal Troon, 2016

Lowest Second Round

63: Mark Hayes, Turnberry, 1977; Greg Norman, Turnberry, 1986; Nick Faldo, Royal St George's, 1993

Lowest Third Round

63: Isao Aoki, Muirfield, 1980; Paul Broadhurst, St Andrews, 1990

Lowest Fourth Round

63: Jodie Mudd, Royal Birkdale, 1991; Payne Stewart, Royal St George's, 1993; Henrik Stenson, Royal Troon, 2016

Lowest Score over the First 36 Holes

130: Nick Faldo, Muirfield, 1992 – 66, 64; Brandt Snedeker, Royal Lytham & St Annes, 2012 – 66, 64

Lowest Score over the Middle 36 Holes

130: Fuzzy Zoeller, Turnberry, 1994 – 66, 64

Lowest Score over the Final 36 Holes

130: Tom Watson, Turnberry, 1977 – 65, 65; Ian Baker-Finch, Royal Birkdale, 1991 – 64, 66; Anders Forsbrand, Turnberry, 1994 – 66, 64; Marc Leishman, St Andrews, 2015 – 64, 66

Lowest Score over the First 54 Holes

198: Tom Lehman, Royal Lytham & St Annes, 1996 – 67, 67, 64
199: Nick Faldo, St Andrews, 1990 – 67, 65, 67; Nick Faldo, Muirfield, 1992 – 66, 64, 69; Adam Scott, Royal Lytham, 2012 – 64, 67, 68

Lowest Score over the Final 54 Holes

196: Henrik Stenson, Royal Troon, 2016 – 65, 68, 63
199: Nick Price, Turnberry, 1994 – 66, 67, 66

Lowest Score for Nine Holes

28: Denis Durnian, first nine, Royal Birkdale, 1983
29: Tom Haliburton, first nine, Royal Lytham & St Annes, 1963; Peter Thomson, first nine, Royal Lytham & St Annes, 1963; Tony Jacklin, first nine, St Andrews, 1970; Bill Longmuir, first nine, Royal Lytham & St Annes, 1979; David J Russell first nine, Royal Lytham & St Annes, 1988; Ian Baker-Finch, first nine, St Andrews, 1990; Paul Broadhurst, first nine, St Andrews, 1990; Ian Baker-Finch, first nine, Royal Birkdale, 1991; Paul McGinley, first nine, Royal Lytham & St Annes, 1996; Ernie Els, first nine, Muirfield, 2002; Sergio Garcia, first nine, Royal Liverpool, 2006; David Lingmerth, first nine, St Andrews, 2015

Most Successive Victories

4: Tommy Morris Jr, 1868-72 (No Championship in 1871)
3: Jamie Anderson, 1877-79; Bob Ferguson, 1880-82; Peter Thomson, 1954-56
2: Tom Morris Sr, 1861-62; JH Taylor, 1894-95; Harry Vardon, 1898-99; James Braid, 1905-06; Bobby Jones, 1926-27; Walter Hagen, 1928-29; Bobby Locke, 1949-50; Arnold Palmer, 1961-62; Lee Trevino, 1971-72; Tom Watson, 1982-83; Tiger Woods, 2005-06; Padraig Harrington, 2007-08

Amateurs Who Have Won The Open

3: Bobby Jones, Royal Lytham & St Annes, 1926; St Andrews, 1927; Royal Liverpool, 1930
2: Harold Hilton, Muirfield, 1892; Royal Liverpool, 1897
1: John Ball Jr, Prestwick, 1890

Champions Who Won on Debut

Willie Park Sr, Prestwick, 1860; Tom Kidd, St Andrews, 1873; Mungo Park, Musselburgh, 1874; Jock Hutchison, St Andrews, 1921; Denny Shute, St Andrews, 1933; Ben Hogan, Carnoustie, 1953; Tony Lema, St Andrews, 1964; Tom Watson, Carnoustie, 1975; Ben Curtis, Royal St George's, 2003

Attendance

Year	Total
1960	39,563
1961	21,708
1962	37,098
1963	24,585
1964	35,954
1965	32,927
1966	40,182
1967	29,880
1968	51,819
1969	46,001
1970	81,593
1971	70,076
1972	84,746
1973	78,810
1974	92,796
1975	85,258
1976	92,021
1977	87,615
1978	125,271
1979	134,501
1980	131,610
1981	111,987
1982	133,299
1983	142,892
1984	193,126
1985	141,619
1986	134,261
1987	139,189
1988	191,334
1989	160,639
1990	208,680
1991	189,435
1992	146,427
1993	141,000
1994	128,000
1995	180,000
1996	170,000
1997	176,000
1998	195,100
1999	157,000
2000	230,000
2001	178,000
2002	161,500
2003	183,000
2004	176,000
2005	223,000
2006	230,000
2007	154,000
2008	201,500
2009	123,000
2010	201,000
2011	180,100
2012	181,300
2013	142,036
2014	202,917
2015	237,024
2016	173,134

Greatest Interval Between First and Last Victory

19 years: JH Taylor, 1894-1913
18 years: Harry Vardon, 1896-1914
15 years: Willie Park Sr, 1860-75; Gary Player, 1959-74
14 years: Henry Cotton, 1934-48

Greatest Interval Between Victories

11 years: Henry Cotton, 1937-48 *(No Championship 1940-45)*
10 years: Ernie Els, 2002-12
9 years: Willie Park Sr, 1866-75; Bob Martin, 1876-85; JH Taylor, 1900-09; Gary Player, 1959-68

Champions Who Have Won in Three Separate Decades

Harry Vardon, 1896, 1898 & 1899/1903/1911 & 1914
JH Taylor, 1894 & 1895/1900 & 1909/1913
Gary Player, 1959, 1968, 1974

Competitors with the Most Top Five Finishes

16: JH Taylor; Jack Nicklaus

Competitors Who Have Recorded the Most Rounds Under Par From 1963

59: Jack Nicklaus
54: Nick Faldo

Competitors with the Most Finishes Under Par From 1963

15: Ernie Els
14: Jack Nicklaus; Nick Faldo
13: Tom Watson

Champions Who Have Led Outright After Every Round

72 hole Championships
Ted Ray, 1912; Bobby Jones, 1927; Gene Sarazen, 1932; Henry Cotton, 1934; Tom Weiskopf, 1973; Tiger Woods, 2005; Rory McIlroy, 2014
36 hole Championships
Willie Park Sr, 1860 and 1866; Tom Morris Sr, 1862 and 1864; Tommy Morris Jr, 1869 and 1870; Mungo Park, 1874; Jamie Anderson, 1879; Bob Ferguson, 1880, 1881, 1882; Willie Fernie, 1883; Jack Simpson, 1884; Hugh Kirkaldy, 1891

Largest Leads Since 1892

After 18 holes:
5 strokes: Sandy Herd, 1896
4 strokes: Harry Vardon, 1902; Jim Barnes, 1925; Christy O'Connor Jr, 1985
After 36 holes:
9 strokes: Henry Cotton, 1934
6 strokes: Abe Mitchell, 1920
After 54 holes:
10 strokes: Henry Cotton, 1934
7 strokes: Harry Vardon, 1903; Tony Lema, 1964
6 strokes: JH Taylor, 1900; James Braid, 1905; James Braid, 1908; Max Faulkner, 1951; Tom Lehman, 1996; Tiger Woods, 2000; Rory McIlroy, 2014

Champions Who Had Four Rounds, Each Better than the One Before

Jack White, Royal St George's, 1904 – 80, 75, 72, 69
James Braid, Muirfield, 1906 – 77, 76, 74, 73
Ben Hogan, Carnoustie, 1953 – 73, 71, 70, 68
Gary Player, Muirfield, 1959 – 75, 71, 70, 68

Same Number of Strokes in Each of the Four Rounds by a Champion

Denny Shute, St Andrews, 1933 – 73, 73, 73, 73 (excluding the play-off)

Best 18-Hole Recovery by a Champion

George Duncan, Deal, 1920. Duncan was 13 strokes behind the leader, Abe Mitchell, after 36 holes and level with him after 54.

Greatest Variation Between Rounds by a Champion

14 strokes: Henry Cotton, 1934, second round 65, fourth round 79
12 strokes: Henry Cotton, 1934, first round 67, fourth round 79
11 strokes: Jack White, 1904, first round 80, fourth round 69; Greg Norman, 1986, first round 74, second round 63; Greg Norman, 1986, second round 63, third round 74
10 strokes: Seve Ballesteros, 1979, second round 65, third round 75

Greatest Variation Between Two Successive Rounds by a Champion

11 strokes: Greg Norman, 1986, first round 74, second round 63; Greg Norman, 1986, second round 63, third round 74
10 strokes: Seve Ballesteros, 1979, second round 65, third round 75

Greatest Comeback by a Champion

After 18 holes
Harry Vardon, 1896, 11 strokes behind the leader
After 36 holes
George Duncan, 1920, 13 strokes behind the leader
After 54 holes
Paul Lawrie, 1999, 10 strokes behind the leader

Champions Who Had Four Rounds Under 70

Greg Norman, Royal St George's, 1993 – 66, 68, 69, 64; Nick Price, Turnberry, 1994 – 69, 66, 67, 66; Tiger Woods, St Andrews, 2000 – 67, 66, 67, 69; Henrik Stenson, Royal Troon, 2016 – 68, 65, 68, 63

Competitors Who Failed to Win The Open Despite Having Four Rounds Under 70

Ernie Els, Royal St George's, 1993 – 68, 69, 69, 68; Jesper Parnevik, Turnberry, 1994 – 68, 66, 68, 67; Ernie Els, Royal Troon, 2004 – 69, 69, 68, 68; Rickie Fowler, Royal Liverpool, 2014 – 69, 69, 68, 67

Lowest Final Round by a Champion

63: Henrik Stenson, Royal Troon, 2016
64: Greg Norman, Royal St George's, 1993
65: Tom Watson, Turnberry, 1977; Seve Ballesteros, Royal Lytham & St Annes, 1988; Justin Leonard, Royal Troon, 1997

Worst Round by a Champion Since 1939

78: Fred Daly, third round, Royal Liverpool, 1947
76: Bobby Locke, second round, Royal St George's, 1949; Paul Lawrie, third round, Carnoustie, 1999

Champion with the Worst Finishing Round Since 1939

75: Sam Snead, St Andrews, 1946

Lowest Opening Round by a Champion

65: Louis Oosthuizen, St Andrews, 2010

Most Open Championship Appearances

46: Gary Player
41: Sandy Lyle
38: Sandy Herd, Jack Nicklaus, Tom Watson
37: Nick Faldo

Most Final Day Appearances Since 1892

32: Jack Nicklaus
31: Sandy Herd
30: JH Taylor
28: Ted Ray
27: Harry Vardon, James Braid, Nick Faldo
26: Peter Thomson, Gary Player, Tom Watson

Most Appearances by a Champion Before His First Victory

19: Darren Clarke, 2011; Phil Mickelson, 2013
15: Nick Price, 1994
14: Sandy Herd, 1902
13: Ted Ray, 1912; Jack White, 1904; Reg Whitcombe, 1938; Mark O'Meara, 1998
11: George Duncan, 1920; Nick Faldo, 1987; Ernie Els, 2002; Stewart Cink, 2009; Zach Johnson, 2015; Henrik Stenson, 2016

The Open Which Provided the Greatest Number of Rounds Under 70 Since 1946

148 rounds, Turnberry, 1994

The Open with the Fewest Rounds Under 70 Since 1946

2 rounds, St Andrews, 1946; Royal Liverpool, 1947; Carnoustie, 1968

Statistically Most Difficult Hole Since 1982

St Andrews, 1984, Par-4 17th, 4.79

Longest Course in Open History

Carnoustie, 2007, 7,421 yards

Number of Times Each Course Has Hosted The Open Championship

St Andrews, 29; Prestwick, 24; Muirfield, 16; Royal St George's, 14; Royal Liverpool, 12; Royal Lytham & St Annes, 11; Royal Birkdale, 9; Royal Troon, 9; Carnoustie, 7; Musselburgh, 6; Turnberry, 4; Royal Cinque Ports, 2; Royal Portrush and Prince's, 1

Prize Money (£)

Year	Total	First Prize	Year	Total	First Prize	Year	Total	First Prize	Year	Total	First Prize
1860	nil	nil	1890	29.50	13	1966	15,000	2,100	1993	1,000,000	100,000
1863	10	nil	1891	28.50	10	1968	20,000	3,000	1994	1,100,000	110,000
1864	15	6	1892	110	35	1969	30,000	4,250	1995	1,250,000	125,000
1865	20	8	1893	100	30	1970	40,000	5,250	1996	1,400,000	200,000
1866	11	6	1900	125	50	1971	45,000	5,500	1997	1,600,000	250,000
1867	16	7	1910	135	50	1972	50,000	5,500	1998	1,800,000	300,000
1868	12	6	1920	225	75	1975	75,000	7,500	1999	2,000,000	350,000
1872	unknown	8	1927	275	75	1977	100,000	10,000	2000	2,750,000	500,000
1873	unknown	11	1930	400	100	1978	125,000	12,500	2001	3,300,000	600,000
1874	20	8	1931	500	100	1979	155,000	15,000	2002	3,800,000	700,000
1876	27	10	1946	1,000	150	1980	200,000	25,000	2003	3,900,000	700,000
1877	20	8	1949	1,500	300	1982	250,000	32,000	2004	4,000,000	720,000
1878	unknown	8	1951	1,700	300	1983	310,000	40,000	2007	4,200,000	750,000
1879	47	10	1953	2,500	500	1984	451,000	55,000	2010	4,800,000	850,000
1880	unknown	8	1954	3,500	750	1985	530,000	65,000	2011	5,000,000	900,000
1881	21	8	1955	3,750	1,000	1986	600,000	70,000	2013	5,250,000	945,000
1882	47.25	12	1958	4,850	1,000	1987	650,000	75,000	2014	5,400,000	975,000
1883	20	8	1959	5,000	1,000	1988	700,000	80,000	2015	6,300,000	1,150,000
1884	23	8	1960	7,000	1,250	1989	750,000	80,000	2016	6,500,000	1,175,000
1885	35.50	10	1961	8,500	1,400	1990	825,000	85,000			
1886	20	8	1963	8,500	1,500	1991	900,000	90,000			
1889	22	8	1965	10,000	1,750	1992	950,000	95,000			

PHOTOGRAPHY CREDITS

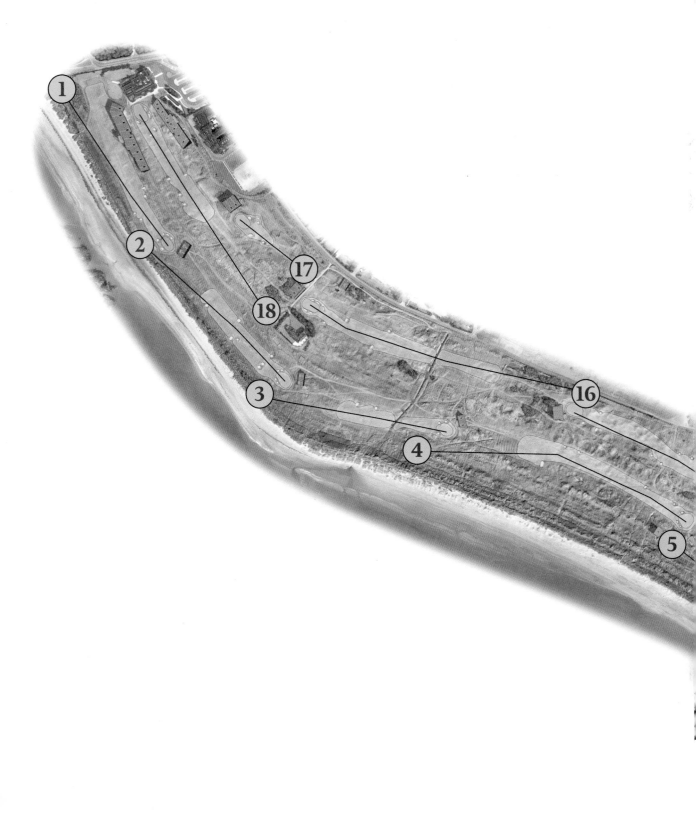